A Bibliography of
ELIZABETH BARRETT BROWNING

A *Bibliography of*

ELIZABETH BARRETT BROWNING

by Warner Barnes

THE UNIVERSITY OF TEXAS & BAYLOR UNIVERSITY

FOR *My Parents*, W.B.

Library of Congress Catalogue Card Number: 67–64500

This publication was made possible by a grant from
the Minnie Stevens Piper Foundation

Published by
THE HUMANITIES RESEARCH CENTER
THE UNIVERSITY OF TEXAS
and
THE ARMSTRONG BROWNING LIBRARY
BAYLOR UNIVERSITY
Distributed by
UNIVERSITY OF TEXAS PRESS
AUSTIN, TEXAS

Printed and bound in the United States of America

CONTENTS

LIST OF ILLUSTRATIONS

Portrait of Elizabeth Barrett Browning
Concealed Impressions in four volumes
"A Curse for a Nation." manuscript page.
Two poems, wrapper
The Runaway Slave at Pilgrim's Point, wrapper
Aurora Leigh, third edition
Sonnets from the Portuguese, title page
A Drama of Exile, Binding variants

INTRODUCTION

THE ONLY DESCRIPTIVE BIBLIOGRAPHY OF ELIZABETH BARRETT BROWN-ing to appear previously was compiled by Thomas J. Wise and printed for private circulation as a limited edition of 100 copies in 1918. In addition to listing over 500 books not included by Wise and supplying information about his own contributions to the Browning canon, the present study through an examination of multiple copies of E. B. B.'s works on the Hinman collator records a heretofore unreported state or impression for all of the author's first editions.

The bibliography is arranged in five parts and three indices: (A) first English editions, authorized first American editions, and those later English editions published within the life of the author containing new material or substantial revision; (B) posthumously printed works, and the forgeries of Wise and his confederates; (C) contributions to periodicals, newspapers, gift books, and anthologies; (D) letters; (E) a short title list of all reprints to the present time. The first index contains an alphabetical list of each of the author's poems with a series of entry numbers representing those English editions in which the poems were reprinted during E.B.B.'s life. Those poems containing *substantive* textual variants are marked with a dagger †. The second index contains an alphabetical list of all book titles with entry numbers in parts A–E. The third index contains a list of printers, publishers, and editors.

The description for books entered in parts A and B contains the following. A quasi-facsimile transcription of the title page including all ornaments, rules, and quotations, except quotations in Greek. Printers of each volume are noted under the heading of *Special imprints*. In the collational line formula the height and width of leaves are given in centimeters. Signatures for English books are described in the conventional way according to Greg's formulary with the use of the Greek letters π and χ to represent preliminary unsigned and inserted gatherings respectively. A full statement of signing appears under the heading of *Typography and paper*. For American books containing double sets of signatures (both numbers and letters), the use of angle brackets $\langle \; \rangle$ has been employed to record that set of signatures not corresponding to the folding of the sheets. Contemporary books which are completely unsigned have their collations enclosed within square brackets and are prefaced with the statement unsigned as [Unsigned 1–3^8 4^6 5–15^8]. For pamphlets of only one unsigned gathering I have adopted the convention established in several of the recent *Soho Bibliographies* of enclosing the letter A within square brackets and indicating the number of leaves in superior figures as [A]^{16}.

Pagination of each book is given in full with unnumbered pages being enclosed in square brackets. The pagination of entirely blank leaves is noted by using italicized arabic numbers within square brackets as [6]. Misnumbered pages are indicated with equal signs as $217 = 219$.

The *Contents* of each book is given in quasi-facsimile transcription with the title of each poem enclosed in single quotation marks. Any editorial comment is enclosed in angle brackets. If a poem has no title, I have quoted the first line and enclosed it in square brackets. Since the *Sonnets from the Portuguese* were never given titles by E.B.B. and their order was changed in the *Poems* of 1856, I have included the first line of each in the contents.

Under the heading *Typography and paper* the symbol $ is used to indicate the number of leaves signed in each gathering. Running titles are given in quasi-facsimile transcription. To indicate the maximum size of the chase I have listed three measurements: the height, both excluding and including the headline and direction line, and the width of the type page as 12.8 (13.8) $\times$ 7.5 cm. At times I have discovered concealed impressions by differences in the gutter margins (the distance between the inner type margins of two conjugate leaves) and several examples of such measurements are listed in each collation. Lastly, I record the thickness of the leaves.

To identify the binding I have used the prose descriptions of publishers' cloth as given in the several books on this subject by John Carter and Michael Sadlier. When possible I have given also the identifying letters used to describe publishers' cloth as found in Jacob Blanck's *Bibliography of American Literature*. Colors designated are those used to describe unfaded cloth observed in natural sunlight. Binders' leaves as distinct from blank leaves of the first or last gathering are noted here with a description of the endpapers. Edges are described as gilded, stained, unopened, or untrimmed. I have not used the term "uncut" because of the popular misunderstanding of its meaning. My investigation of inserted publishers' catalogues reflects the opinion of other bibliographers that these have no relationship to the priority of the sheets within the several impressions of a given edition. And it should come as no surprise that in E.B.B.'s *Poems* of 1844, I locate a copy of the second impression with a June catalogue and a first impression with an August catalogue.

The *Notes* provide information on the date of publication of the book, the price, and when known the number of copies in the edition. Unfortunately the publishers' records for her earlier books are no longer extant and these dates of publication have been obtained from contemporary advertisements in the trade papers and periodicals. If known, the location of manuscripts, page proofs, or copies containing corrections in the hand of the author are given. Pertinent details of the forgeries of Thomas J. Wise are included in part B.

My use of the terms state, issue, impression, and edition correspond to those suggested in Fredson Bowers' *Principles of Bibliographical Description*. I use one additional term, variant, to describe typographical differences not caused by deliberate resetting, but by the accidental slipping of type in the chase. The priority of variants is indicated by my use of terms *first, second,* or *third*. If I am uncertain of the priority, I use the letters A, B, and C, and no sequence should be inferred.

All first English editions were machine collated with an average of six copies being compared for each book. One of my colleagues has remarked recently that many old time bookmen have an aversion to this kind of analysis, but the results of the research are self evident: a variant state or concealed impression was discovered for every volume so examined. In addition to textual variants I have described another kind of evidence for discovering concealed impressions, the width of the type page. Early in my collation I began to notice that some of the pages within a given gathering would not superimpose laterally in the viewing box of the collator. My first reaction was that the tables of the machine upon which the two books rested simply were misaligned. However as this pattern began to emerge with some regularity, I started to measure the width of the type pages. In those instances in which lateral superimposition of the pages could not be obtained, a measurement of the type pages indicated a difference in width from 0.5 to 1.5 millimeters. I ruled out paper shrinkage as an explanation, for it is not logical that some pages within a gathering should show different measurements whereas other pages should show no difference at all. Nor does it stand to reason that there should be a difference in the width of two type pages, but no difference in the length. Further examination of additional copies at other libraries confirmed these results. The explanation to me lies in the varying amount of pressure placed upon the type from one impression to the next while it is locked up in the chase, a procedure which can be empirically verified on any hand press today. I have given three examples of the difference in type page width for each concealed impression, although on most occasions more examples were observed. The point measured in each instance was the widest line on the page. At no time have I concluded that this difference alone and in itself furnished evidence establishing concealed impressions, but there is no book I examined in which evidence of resetting did not occur simultaneously with a difference in type page width.

For each variant, be it a binding state or concealed impression, I have located one copy. The library location symbols used throughout the bibliography for English libraries are taken from Donald Wing's *Short Title Catalogue of Books . . . 1641 to 1700*. For American libraries I have used the symbols which appear in the *National Union Catalogue of The Library of Congress*. For several libraries not listed in either of these works I have supplied my own symbols: Le = The University of Leeds; Liv = The University of Liverpool; DCP = The Public Library of the District of Columbia. Books from my own collection are entered as WB.

The list in part E contains all known reprintings to the present time except undated stereotyped reimpressions. This was compiled by asking over 100 libraries throughout the world to report omissions to a preliminary checklist compiled from *The National Union Catalogue, The British Museum Catalogue of Printed Books*, and the catalogue of the Boldeian Library. Where possible I have located three copies of each book; entries containing fewer than three copies may indicate a relative scarcity. At least one copy of each book in this section has been examined, or I have seen photocopy of it unless noted to the contrary. Entries do not present a quasi-facsimile transcription of the title page, but instead give a short title with an abbreviated form of the publisher's imprint.

This bibliography at once will suggest several areas for future research. First, a complete list of all translations of E.B.B.'s works should be compiled, for with the exception of *Sonnets from the Portuguese* I have excluded all works printed in languages other than English. This decision was made with reluctance. However only six of her other translations are held in total by the British Museum and the Bodleian and only eight are recorded in *The National Union Catalogue*. No editions in non-European languages are catalogued by any library I visited. Rather than to enter books from dealers' catalogues and such sources as the *Index Translationam* which I have not seen and to include only a small part of the whole, it seems better to defer translations to another investigator.

Second, recent critical and biographical studies have not taken into account the numerous textual revisions made by the author to her poems as they passed from one edition to another. On the other hand by ignoring W. W. Greg's classic distinction between substantives and accidentals, some critics have erroneously assumed that *any* change in punctuation is a *bona fide* authorial revision. As a footnote to textual study it is ironic that in not one of the many reprintings of the *Sonnets from the Portuguese* has the text been established, for none present the changes made by E.B.B. in the *Poems* of 1853 and 1856 while retaining the accidentals of the sonnets' first appearance in the *Poems* of 1850.

Third, collation of the *Poems* of 1856, the last edition to appear within the author's lifetime, with the posthumously published editions of 1862 and 1864 reveals no substantive changes were made. However Chapman and Hall used a different printer for these later editions, and a new house style was imposed upon the text, resulting on the average in a change of five to six accidental textual variants per page. Unfortunately posthumously published works were used as a text for the first 'complete' edition edited by Kenyon in 1897, and almost all modern reprints descend from this work. However in Kenyon's edition not only is there a new set of accidentals imposed upon the text, but it was further corrupted by the introduction of many unauthorized substantive changes. To establish the text for the entire works of Nineteenth Century England's most popular woman poet remains a *desideratum*. Towards the preparation of a definitive edition I hope the material in my first index will provide a guide.

Fourth, contrary to the opinion of Professors Wellek and Warren in their *Theory of Literature* that Thomas J. Wise never manufactured a literary text, and that therefore his activities are of interest only to the book collector, not the critic, the collations I have included reveal that what he intended to pass off as the first published appearances of the *Sonnets from the Portuguese* and *The Runaway Slave at Pilgrim's Point* were versions never written by Elizabeth Barrett Browning.

One word more. I am aware of no bibliography yet published for which errors and omissions have not been reported, and I am sure that this work will prove no exception. In fact, I am confident that if more than six copies of E.B.B.'s editions are subjected to machine collation, still further concealed impressions than are here recorded shall be discovered. There has been an unfortunate tendency of late by some American bibliographers to assume that every variant of every book has been seen by them and that surely no copy exists anywhere else which might provide additional information. Time has and will prove any such assumption false. What a bibliography should do is to provide descriptions to admit the undertaking of further research. If my book is accepted in this way, I will feel it has been received in the spirit in which it was intended.

IOWA CITY, *December, 1965*

ACKNOWLEDGMENTS

FIRST, TO JACK HERRING, DIRECTOR OF THE ARMSTRONG BROWNING Library, I extend my thanks for his many kindnesses and the attention he has given the publication of this bibliography since its inception. His librarian, Mrs. L. E. Wood and his assistant Kenneth King, have spent countless hours wrapping and mailing packages of books to me and for this I am indebted. Much of the machine collation was done in the Stark Library at The University of Texas, and I wish to acknowledge my appreciation to Mrs. June Moll and Mrs. Elise Shoemaker. At the University of Iowa Library many tasks were performed in my behalf by Dale Bentz, Frank Hanlin, Frank Paluka, and Ronald Fingerson. At Oxford Desmond Neill at the Bodleian and E. V. Quinn at Balliol kindly allowed me to examine the books at their disposal and offered suggestions in exploring new avenues of research. At Cornell George Harris Healey provided assistance on several occasions. To Warren Roberts of the University of Texas my sincere thanks for seeing the book through production.

The following libraries and librarians have patiently answered questions, sent books, and photocopied material in their collections. It is to them that the credit should go for furnishing evidence to

verify many of the imprints in this book: Arizona State University
Library, Jerold A. Nelson; Boston College, Bapst Library; Boston
Public Library, John Alden; Boston University, Cherney Library;
Brown University Library, Christine D. Hathaway, Elizabeth C.
Wescott; Bryn Mawr College Library, Janet M. Agnew; Columbia
University, Butler Library, Eugene P. Sheehy; Duke University
Library, Florence Blakely; Dartmouth College, Baker Memorial
Library, Priscilla Page; District of Columbia Public Library, Rich-
ard G. Hunt; Durham University Library; Edinburgh University
Library; Emory University Library, Ruth Walling; Enoch Pratt
Free Library, Richard Hart; Harvard University Library; Indiana
University Library; Lilly Library, David Randall; Joint University
Libraries Nashville, Tennessee; Lehigh University Library, Anne
Flannery; Liverpool University Library; Louisiana State Univer-
sity Library, Richard Klenk; Newberry Library, James E. Wells;
New York Public Library, Lewis Stark, New York Public Library,
the Berg Collection; Northwestern University Library, Noel A. S.
Evans; Pierpont Morgan Library, D. Ewing; Princeton University
Library, Charles H. Burkman, Marcia Tuttle; Purdue University
Libraries, Esther Schlundt; Scripps College Library, Mary Allely;
Stanford University Library, Julius P. Barclay; Syracuse Univer-
sity Library; The Catholic University of America Library, Thomas
V. Schmidt; The Honnold Library, Esther E. Sweeney; The John
Rylands Library, Ronald Hall; The Johns Hopkins University Li-
brary, M. Hubbard; The Library of Congress; The Ohio State Uni-
versity Library; The Pennsylvania State University Library, Frank
Rodgers; The University of Arizona Library, Ronald L. Sparks; The
University of Chicago Library, Annette Fern; The University of
Florida Libraries, Annette Liles; The University of Georgia Li-
braries, Vivian B. Phillips; The University of Nebraska Library;
The University of North Carolina Library, Louise Hall, Eileen
McIlvaine; The University of Oklahoma Library, Melville R.
Spence; The University of Wisconsin, The Memorial Library; Trin-
ity College Library, Dublin, Hilary Pyle; Tulane University,
Howard-Tilton Memorial Library, Dorothy Whittemore; University of Alabama Library, Peggy J. Duckworth; University of Ar-
kansas General Library; University of California, Berkeley; University of California, Los Angeles; University of Colorado Libraries, Rosemary Lane; University of Kentucky, Margret I. King
Library, Kate Irvine; University of London Library, A. H. Wesen-
craft, M. H. Stothan; University of Maryland Library; University
of Minnesota, Walter Library, Norma Hovden; University of Miss-
ouri Library, Mrs. Ann Todd Rubey; University of Notre Dame,
Memorial Library; University of Oregon Library, Elizabeth
Findly; University of Pittsburg Library; University of South Caro-

lina, McKissick Memorial Library; University of Utah Libraries, Barbara H. Whitaker; University of Virginia Library; University of Washington Library, Curtis W. Stucki; Washington University, John M. Olin Library; Wellesley College Library, Richard Chamberlin, Hannah French; Yale University Library, John A. Braswell, Herman W. Liebert. Also I am indebted to Edward Tripp of the Thomas Y. Crowell Company, the Peter Pauper Press, and Elizabeth Bower of Bradbury and Agnew for making certain information in their publisher's records available to me.

The Graduate College of The University of Iowa has subsidized certain aspects of my research, and the American Council of Learned Societies gave me a grant-in-aid to go to England in the summer of 1964 to examine several Browning collections there. The Piper Foundation of San Antonio, Texas has partly underwritten the printing of the book, and to them I am indeed grateful.

In the Department of English at Iowa John C. Gerber and Curt Zimansky have encouraged my investigations, and without their help my activities could not have been completed. William B. Todd, Director of Bibliographical Research at The University of Texas, and O. M. Brack of Iowa have read my manuscript and offered friendly advice, but any errors which may be discovered are mine, not theirs. Finally I salute my wife who for several summers and countless evenings endured my absence to allow me to compile this work.

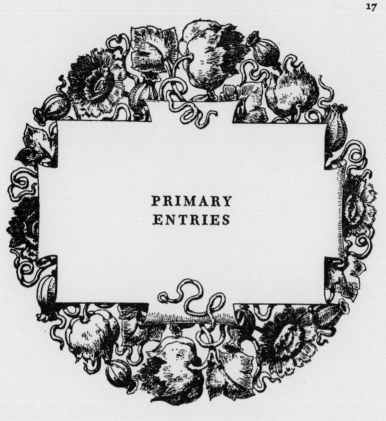

PRIMARY
ENTRIES

A : FIRST ENGLISH EDITIONS

AUTHORIZED FIRST AMERICAN EDITIONS

LATER ENGLISH EDITIONS PUBLISHED

IN LIFETIME OF THE AUTHOR,

CONTAINING NEW MATERIAL

OR SUBSTANTIAL REVISION

A1 : The Battle of Marathon 1820

THE | BATTLE OF MARATHON. | A POEM. | [*fine rule 2.8
cm.*] | —— "Behold | What care employs me now, my vows I pay |
To the sweet Muses, teachers of my youth!" | AKENSIDE. | "An-
cient of days! August Athena! Where, | Where are thy men of
might, thy grand in soul? | Gone—glimmering through the dream
of things that were. | First in the race that led to glory's goal, | They
won, and past away." BYRON. | [*fine rule 2.8 cm.*] | BY E. B. BAR-
RETT. | [*thick rule, thin rule 1.3 cm.*] | 𝕷𝖔𝖓𝖉𝖔𝖓: | PRINTED FOR
W. LINDSELL, 87, WIMPOLE- | STREET, CAVENDISH-
SQUARE. | [*short rule 1.1 cm.*] | 1820.

Special imprints: (p. [ii] at the foot) Printed by Gold and Wal-
ton, | 24 Wardour-street, Soho.

Collation: 22.0 × 14.3 cm; π^8 A–D^8 E^4; 44 leaves.

Pagination: [i–v] vi–xv [xvi], [1] 2–17 [18–21] 22–37 [38–41]
42–56 [57–59] 60–72.

Contents: [i] title page; [ii] printer's imprint; [iii] 10 line dedica-
tion to her father signed 'ELIZABETH B. BARRETT | *Hope End*,
1819'; [iv] blank; [v] 'PREFACE.'; [xvi] blank; [1] 'BOOK I.';
[18] blank; [19] fly title 'BOOK II.'; [20] blank; 21 text; [38]
blank; [39] fly title 'BOOK III.'; [40] blank; [41] text; [57] fly
title 'BOOK IV.'; [58] blank; [59] text; 72 'THE END.'

Typography and paper: $1,2,3,(-B2)$ signed at center of foot. Running titles set in rom. caps. pp. vi–xv as 'PREFACE.', absent elsewhere in text. Pagination set in outer margin of the headline in
the preface; in the text centered at the top of the page. Text irregular, 24 lines + headline and direction line. Leaf A3^r type page
measures 13.4 (14.6) × 83 cm. Gutter margins measure, pp. viii–ix
= 4.5 cm; 68–69 = 4.8 cm; 24–25 = 4.5 cm. White wove paper
watermarked 1818. Sheets bulk 0.6 cm.

Binding: Issued stitched unbound. Three stab holes at inner margin. All copies rebound except that in the Ashley Library.

Notes: Privately printed, not published in an edition of fifty copies
by Elizabeth's father, Edward Barrett. The earliest presentation
copies extant are those at the Huntington and Pierpont Morgan
Libraries dated March 6, 1820. Two manuscripts of the work are
at The University of Texas; one dated 1817, the other 1819. The
following revisions are present in the British Museum copy and

almost all are present also in the copy at the Newberry Library, both presumably in the hand of the author:

4.10	beware	beware,
5.10	convinc'd	convinc'd,
6.4	then	than
8.1	felt	felt,
10.14	give	give,
10.18	Grecian	Grecian's
11.18	Oft	Off
12.2	reared	reared,
12.8	die	die,
13.21	bore	bore,
14.8	sake	sake!
14.16	sky	sky,
15.4	Rome.	Rome."
16.2	bestow,	bestow!"
16.9	flies	flies,
22.13	Oh	"Oh
23.9	rose	rose,
33.18	wall.	wall."
33.21	Not	"Not
34.8	rest	rest."
36.15	stole	stole,
37.6	oceans	ocean
46.6	grave,	grave;
54.1	Assembled	"Assembled
61.24	Perfidious	"Perfidious
62.20	dart	dart,
65.3	glows	glows,

In the errata list provided by Thomas J. Wise and his confederates in their facsimile printing of this book in 1891 and later in Wise's bibliography of E.B.B., only three of these changes are reported and only one made to the text itself. All are easily seen, of course, in Wise's own Ashley library copy from which the facsimile was printed. To provide a facsimile as much like the original as possible for their own particular purposes seems more likely than their expressed intention not to "interfere with small matters of spelling and pointing."

Two variants

A. As described with the following point. Line 11, page [iii] reads 'E. B. BARRETT. (MWelC)
B. As described with this variant. Line 11, page [iii] reads 'E. B. BARRE TT'. (L) Other copies show intermediate spacing

between the letters E and T indicating that the type has slipped in the chase.

Copies examined: MWelC MH NN CtY ICN TxU L CLU–C CSmH.

Copy held: NNPM

A2 : An Essay on Mind 1826

AN | ESSAY ON MIND, | WITH | *OTHER POEMS.* | "BRAMA ASSAI, POCO SPERA, E NULLA CHIEDE." | *Tasso.* | LON-DON: | JAMES DUNCAN, PATERNOSTER-ROW. | MDCCC-XXVI.

Special imprints: (p. [ii] at the foot) Printed by A. Macintosh, Great New-street, London. (p. 152 at the foot) imprint as above.

Collation: 19.2 × 11.1 cm; A⁸ B–G¹² H⁴; 84 leaves.

Pagination: [i–iii] iv–xiii [xiv–xvi], [1–3] 4 [5] 6–42 [43–45] 46 [47] 48–88 [89] 90–97 [98] 99–106 [107–109] 110–111 [112] 113 [114] 115–116 [117] 118–119 [120] 121–122 [123] 124–125 [126] 127–128 [129] 130–131 [132] 133 [134] 135–136 [137] 138 [139] 140–142 [143] 144–145 [146] 147–152.

Contents: [i] title page; [ii] printer's imprint; [iii] 'PREFACE.'; [xiv] blank; [xv] 'CONTENTS.'; [xvi] blank; [1] fly title 'AN | ESSAY ON MIND. | BOOK I. | [*rule*] | "My narrow leaves cannot in them contayne | The large discourse."—SPENSER.'; [2] blank; [3] '*Analysis of the First Book.*'; [5] text; [43] fly title 'AN | ESSAY ON MIND. | BOOK II.'; [44] blank; [45] '*Analysis of the Second Book.*'; [47] text; [89] 'NOTES TO BOOK I.'; [98] 'NOTES TO BOOK II.'; [107] fly title 'MISCELLANEOUS POEMS.'; [108] blank; [109] 'TO MY FATHER ON HIS BIRTH-DAY.'; [112] 'SPENSERIAN STANZAS | ON A BOY OF THREE YEARS OLD.'; [114] 'VERSES TO MY BROTHER.'; [117] 'STANZAS ON THE DEATH OF LORD BYRON.'; [120] 'MEMORY.'; [123] 'TO ————.'; [126] 'STANZAS | *Occasioned by a passage in Mr. Emerson's Journal* . . .'; [129] 'THE PAST.'; [132] 'THE PRAYER.'; [134] 'ON A PICTURE OF RIEGO'S WIDOW, | PLACED IN THE EXHIBITION.'; [137] 'SONG.'; [139] 'THE DREAM. | A FRAGMENT.'; [143] 'RIGA'S LAST SONG.'; [146] 'THE VISION OF FAME.'; 152 'FINIS.', printer's imprint.

Typography and paper: $1,2,5(–A5) signed at center of foot. Leaves B5 C5 D5 E5 F5 G5 signed B3 C3 D3 E3 F3 G3. Running titles set in rom. caps. over a double rule as 'AN ESSAY ON MIND.' or with the titles of the individual poems. Pagination set in the outer margin of the headline. Text irregular, 18 lines + headline and direction line. Leaf E5^r type page measures 10.9 (12.8) × 7.2 cm. Gutter margin measurements vary according to impression. See note below. White wove paper unwatermarked. Sheets bulk 1.0 cm.

Binding: Drab paper boards, printed paper label on spine: '[*two rules*] | ESSAY | ON | MIND | WITH | OTHER | 𝔓oems· | [*short rule*] | 5s bds. | [*two rules*].' White wove end papers. Four stab holes at inner margin. Top and fore edges unopened; bottom edge untrimmed. In the front of some copies a publisher's catalogue of 12 pages dated April, 1826 is inserted. Also, at back in some copies is a prospectus of 8 pages advertising 'THE MODERN TRAVELLER.' (ICN)

Binding variants: Blue paper covered boards, printed paper label as above. (NN)
Drab paper boards, blue paper shelfback. Printed paper label as above. (TxWB)
Drab paper boards, blue diaper cloth shelfback, printed paper label as above. (TxU)

Notes: Published March 25, 1826 at five shillings. The manuscript of "An Essay on Mind" is at the University of Texas.

First Impression

As described with the following points: Page numbers 12, 24, 148 are perfectly aligned. Line 15 page 75 reads '. . . found . . .'. The height of type page 83 is 10.9 cm. Gutter margins measure, pp. 12–13 = 2.6 cm; 84–85 = 2.6 cm; 148–149 = 2.4 cm. (TxU Hanley copy 2)

Second impression

As described with these variants: Page numbers 12, 24, 148 are misaligned. Line 15 page 75 reads '. . . fo und . . .'. The height of type page 83 is 10.8 cm. Gutter margins measure, pp. 12–13 = 3.3 cm; 84–85 = 2.9 cm; 148–149 = 3.0 cm. (TxU Stark)

Copies with mixed sheets can occur in 32 possible combinations. Following is a list of several: Page number 12 aligned, 24 and 148 misaligned; page 83 measures 10.9 cm; line 15, page 75 reads "fo und" (TxWB Boyd). Page numbers 12 and 24 misaligned, 148 aligned; page 83 measures 10.8 cm; line 15, page 75 reads "found" (TxU Wrenn). Page numbers 12 and 24 aligned, 148 misaligned; page 83 measures 10.8 cm; line 15 page 75 reads "fo und" (TxU

Hanley copy 1). The width of the type pages vary in the two impressions but is less than 1 millimeter in each instance noted.

Copies examined: MH MB MWelC NN CtY DLC IU ICN TxU TxWB L O CSmH CLU–C.

A3 : **Prometheus Bound 1833**

PROMETHEUS BOUND. | TRANSLATED FROM THE GREEK | OF ÆSCHYLUS. | AND MISCELLANEOUS POEMS, | BY THE TRANSLATOR, | AUTHOR OF "AN ESSAY ON MIND," WITH OTHER POEMS. | [*short rule 1.8 cm*] | [*one line in Greek*] | MIMNERMUS. | [*one line in Greek*] | THEOGNIS. | [*french rule 1.8 cm*] | LONDON: | PRINTED AND PUBLISHED BY A. J. VALPY, M.A. | RED LION COURT, FLEET STREET. | 1833.

Special imprints: (p. [164] at the foot) PRINTED BY A. J. VALPY, | RED LION COURT, FLEET STREET.

Collation: 18.4 × 11.0 cm; a²x¹b¹⁰ A–F ¹² G¹⁰; 95 leaves.

Pagination: [i–v] vi–xxi [xxii–xxiii] xxiv [xxv–xxvi], [1] 2–68 [69] 70–78 [79–81] 82–92 [93] 94–101 [102] 103–108 [109] 110–112 [113] 114–116 [117] 118–121 [122] 123–125 [126] 127–130 [131] 132–133 [134] 135–136 [137] 138–139 [140] 141–143 [144] 145–146 [147–148] 149–150 [151] 152–155 [156] 157–158 [159] 160–161 [162] 163 [164].

Contents: [i] half title 'PROMETHEUS BOUND. | TRANSLATED FROM THE GREEK | OF ÆSCHYLUS. | AND MISCELLANEOUS POEMS.'; [ii] blank; [iii] title page; [iv] blank; [v] 'PREFACE.'; [xxii] blank; [xxiii] 'CONTENTS.'; [xxv] fly title 'PROMETHEUS BOUND.'; [xxvi] 'PERSONS OF THE DRAMA.'; [1] text; [69] 'NOTES TO PROMETHEUS BOUND.'; [79] fly title 'MISCELLANEOUS POEMS.'; [80] blank; [81] 'THE TEMPEST. | A FRAGMENT.'; [93] 'A SEA-SIDE MEDITATION.'; [102] 'A VISION OF LIFE AND DEATH.'; [109] 'EARTH.'; [113] 'THE PICTURE GALLERY AT PENSHURST.'; [117] 'TO A POET'S CHILD.'; [122] 'MINSTRELSY.'; [126] 'TO THE MEMORY OF | SIR UVEDALE PRICE, BART.'; [131] 'THE AUTUMN.'; [134] 'THE DEATH-BED OF TERESA DEL RIEGO.'; [137] 'TO VICTOIRE, ON HER MARRIAGE.'; [140] 'TO A BOY.'; [144] 'REMONSTRANCE.'; [147] 'EPITAPH.'; [148] 'THE IMAGE OF GOD.'; [151] 'THE APPEAL.'; [156]

'IDOLS.'; [159] 'HYMN.'; [162] 'WEARINESS.'; [163] 'THE END.'; [164] printer's imprint.

Typography and paper: $1 signed centered at the foot. Running titles set in rom. caps. with the titles of the individual works as 'PROMETHEUS BOUND.' Pages 70–77 read 'NOTES TO | PROMETHEUS BOUND.' but page 78 reads 'NOTES TO PROM-ETHEUS BOUND.' Pagination set in the outer margin of the headline. Text irregular, 19 lines + headline and direction line. Leaf C1^r type page measures 11.4 (12.8) × 7.6 cm. Gutter margins measure, pp. 12–13 = 3.5 cm; 60–61 = 2.5 cm; 84–85 = 2.7 cm. On page 90 line 10 the fifth and sixth asterisks have fallen out of line. White wove paper unwatermarked. Sheets bulk 1.2 cm.

Binding: Blue watered silk (AA) cloth. No stamping on the sides. Printed paper label on spine: '[*thick rule, thin rule*] | PROME-THEUS BOUND, | AND MISCELLANEOUS POEMS. | Price 5s. | [*thin rule, thick rule*]'. White wove end papers. Four stab holes at inner margin. Top and fore edges unopened; bottom edge trimmed.

Remainder binding: Brown paper covered boards. Printed paper label on spine: '[*thick rule, thin rule*] | PROMETHEUS | BOUND, | AND | OTHER POEMS. | [*rule*] | E. BARRETT. | [*thin rule, thick rule*]'. (OB)

Notes: Published May 11, 1833 at five shillings. The manuscript of "Prometheus Bound" is at The University of Texas.

First state

As described with the following point: Line 13 page 154 reads "... tongues ,that". (TxWB)

Second state

As described with this variant: Line 13 page 154 corrected to read "... tongues, that". (TxU)

Copies examined: MH MWelC MB NN DLC CtY IU ICN TxU TxWB L O OB CLU–C.

A4 : The Seraphim 1838

THE SERAPHIM, | AND | OTHER POEMS. | BY | ELIZABETH B. BARRETT, | AUTHOR OF | A TRANSLATION OF THE "PROMETHEUS BOUND," &c. | Some to sing, and some to say, | Some to weep, and some to praye. | SKELTON. | LONDON: | SAUNDERS AND OTLEY, CONDUIT STREET. | 1838.

Special imprints: (p. [ii] at the center) LONDON: | PRINTED BY SAMUEL BENTLEY, | Dorset Street, Fleet Street. (p. 360 at the foot) LONDON: PRINTED BY SAMUEL BENTLEY, | Dorset Street, Fleet Street.

Collation: 19.1 × 11.0 cm; A–Q^{12}; 192 leaves.

Pagination: [2] [i–v] vi–xviii [xix] xx–xxi [xxii], [1–3] 4–25 [26–29] 30–78 [79–81] 82–89 [90–91] 92–99 [100–101] 102–103 [104–105] 106–109 [110–111] 112–118 [119–121] 122–135 [136–139] 140–170 [171–173] 174–184 [185] 186–198 [199] 200–206 [207] 208–220 [221] 222–229 [230–231] 232–238 [239] 240–252 [253] 254–263 [264–265] 266–270 [271] 272–275 [276–277] 278–281 [282–283] 284–286 [287] 288–289 [290] 291–292 [293] 294–296 [297] 298–300 [301] 302–306 [307] 308 [309] 310–313 [314] 315–317 [318] 319–320 [321] 322 [323] 324–327 [328] 329–331 [332] 333–334 [335–337] 338–339 [340] 341 [342] 343 [344] 345 [346] 347–353 [354] 355 [356] 357–360.

Contents: 1 blank leaf; [i] half title 'THE SERAPHIM | AND | OTHER POEMS.'; [ii] printer's imprint; [iii] title page; [iv] blank; [v] 'PREFACE.' dated 'LONDON, 1838.'; [xix] 'CONTENTS.'; [xxii] blank; [1] fly-title 'THE SERAPHIM. | PART THE FIRST. | [*rule*] | [two line quotation in Greek]. ORPHEUS. | "I look for angels' songs, and hear Him cry." | GILES FLETCHER.'; [2] blank; [3] text; [26] blank; [27] fly title 'THE SERAPHIM. | PART THE SECOND. | [*rule*] | two line quotation in Greek] | CHRYSOSTOM. | [five line quotation] | SPENSER.'; [28] blank; [29] text; [79] fly title 'THE POET'S VOW | [*rule*] | —O be wiser thou, | Instructed that true knowledge leads to love. | WORDSWORTH.'; [80] blank; [81] 'THE POET'S VOW. | PART THE FIRST.'; 90 blank; [91] 'THE POET'S VOW. | PART THE SECOND.'; [100] blank; [101] 'THE POET'S VOW. | PART THE THIRD.'; [104] blank; [105] 'THE POET'S VOW. | PART THE FOURTH.'; [110] blank; [111] 'THE POET'S VOW. | PART THE FIFTH.'; [119] fly title 'THE ROMAUNT OF MARGARET. | [*rule*] | Can my affections find out nothing best | But still and still remove ?— | QUARLES.'; [120] blank; [121] text; [136] blank; [137] fly title 'ISOBEL'S CHILD. | [*rule*] | — so find we profit, | By losing of our prayers. | SHAKESPEARE.'; [138] blank; [139] text; [171] fly title 'A ROMANCE OF THE GANGES. | [*rule*] | [three line quotation] | TENNYSON.'; [172] blank; [173] text; [185] 'THE ISLAND.'; [199] 'THE DESERTED GARDEN.'; [207] 'THE SOUL'S TRAVELLING.'; [221] 'SOUNDS.'; [230] blank; [231] 'NIGHT AND THE MERRY MAN.'; [239] 'EARTH AND HER PRAISERS.'; [253] 'THE VIRGIN MARY TO THE |

CHILD JESUS.'; [264] blank; [265] 'STANZAS TO BETTINE, |
THE FRIEND OF GOETHE.'; [271] 'STANZAS ON THE
DEATH | OF MRS. HEMANS, | WRITTEN IN REFERENCE
TO MISS LANDON'S POEM | ON THE SAME SUBJECT.';
[276] blank; [277] 'MEMORY AND HOPE.'; [282] blank; [283]
'THE SLEEP.'; [287] MAN AND NATURE.'; [290] 'THE SEA-
SIDE WALK.'; [293] 'THE SEA-MEW.'; [297] 'THE LITTLE
FRIEND.'; [301] 'MY DOVES.'; [307] 'TO MISS MITFORD | IN
HER GARDEN.'; [309] 'THE STUDENT.'; [314] 'THE EXILE'S
RETURN.'; [318] 'A SONG AGAINST SINGING | TO MY
DEAR LITTLE COUSIN | ELIZABETH JANE H—.'; [321]
'STANZAS.'; [323] 'THE YOUNG QUEEN.'; [328] 'VIC-
TORIA'S TEARS.'; [332] 'VANITIES.'; [335] 'BEREAVEMENT.';
[336] 'CONSOLATION,'; [337] 'A SUPPLICATION FOR
LOVE | HYMN I.'; [340] 'THE MEDIATOR. | HYMN II.'; [342]
'THE WEEPING SAVIOUR. | HYMN III.'; [344] 'THE MEAS-
URE. | HYMN IV.'; [346] 'COWPER'S GRAVE.'; [354] 'THE
WEAKEST THING.'; [356] 'THE NAME.'; 360 'THE END.',
printer's imprint.

Typography and paper: $1,2,5(-A2)$ signed toward outer margin
of foot. Running titles set in rom. caps. with the titles of the individual poems as 'A SONG AGAINST SINGING.' Pagination set in
outer margin of the headline. Text irregular, 19 lines + headline
and direction line. Leaf El^r type page measures 11.5 (12.9) × 7.5
cm. Gutter margins measure, pp. 156–157 = 3.9 cm; 180–181 = 3.0
cm; 252–[253] = 3.7 cm. The running title on page 317 reads 'THE
EXILE,S RETURN,'. White wove paper unwatermarked. Sheets
bulk 2.5 cm.

Binding: Claret diaper cloth. Sides blind stamped with a scroll and
feather design. Spine: '[*ornament*] | THE | SERAPHIM | AND |
OTHER POEMS | [*ornament*].' All in gilt. Yellow coated end
papers. Also peach coated end papers. Four stab holes at inner
margin. Top and fore edges unopened; bottom edge untrimmed.
(NN) Also, in claret ripple grain (TZ) cloth with the same stamping. Spine as above. (O)

Binding variants: Claret morocco-like (AR) cloth. Sides blind
stamped with a frame of six rules enclosing an oval design of six
leaves. Spine as above. (ICU) Also in claret close grain diaper
(H) cloth with the same stamping (MWelC).

Claret small grain (H) diaper cloth. Sides blind stamped with a
frame of four rules enclosing a rectangular design of flowers and
leaves. Spine as above. (NN Berg)

Claret vertically ribbed (T) cloth. Sides blind stamped with a frame of two rules enclosing an arabesque design. Spine as above (L). Also in claret small grain (H) diaper cloth with the same stamping. (CtY)

Blue small grain (H) diaper cloth. No stamping on sides. Spine: '[*two rules*] | BARRETT'S | SERAPHIM | &c. | [*two rules*]'. All in gilt. (DLC)

Notes: Published June 6, 1838 at seven shillings and six-pence.

First impression

As described with the following points: Line 1 page [ii] reads 'LONDON :'. Leaf A5^r and leaf A6^r are both signed 'A5'. The words "Toward the sea," line 15, page 214 are set flush with the outer type margin. Page 60 type page measure vertically 11.5 cm. (TxU Aitken)

Second impression

As described with these variants: Line 1 page [ii] reads 'LON-DON:' Only leaf A5^r signed 'A5'. The words "Toward the sea." page 214, line 15 have been reset and are not flush with the outer margin. Page 60 an extra lead has been inserted following line 16 and the type page measures vertically 11.5 cm. (TxU Wrenn)

The width of several type pages in the two impressions as follows:

page line	1st	2nd
[3].16	7.6	7.5
21.1	7.6	7.5
54.7	7.5	7.4

Copies examined: MH MB MWelC NN DLC CtY IU IaU ICN ICU TxU TxWB L O CSmH.

A5 : Poems 1844

POEMS. | BY | ELIZABETH BARRETT BARRETT, | AUTHOR OF "THE SERAPHIM," ETC. | [*rule 1.0 cm.*] | "De patrie, et de Dieu, des poètes, de l'âme | Qui s'élève en priant." —VICTOR HUGO. | [*rule 1.0 cm.*] | IN TWO VOLUMES. | VOL. I. [II.] | LONDON: | EDWARD MOXON, DOVER STREET. | MDCCC-XLIV.

Special imprints: Vol. 1 (p. [ii] at the center) LONDON: | BRADBURY AND EVANS, PRINTERS, WHITEFRIARS. (p. 250 at the foot) imprint as above Vol. 2 (p. [ii] at the center) and (p. [276] at the foot) imprint as above.

Collation: Vol. 1 17.2 × 10.4 cm; a⁸ B–Q⁸ R⁶; 134 leaves. Vol. 2 17.2 × 10.4 cm; [A]² B–S⁸ T²; 140 leaves.

Pagination: Vol. 1 [i–iii] iv [v] vi–xiv [xv] xvi, [1–3] 4–119 [120–123] 124–150 [151–152] 153–170 [171–172] 173–250 [251–252]. Vol. 2 [i–iii] iv, [1–3] 4–59 [60–63] 64–275 [276].

Contents: Vol. 1 [i] title page; [ii] printer's imprint; [iii] 'Dedication. | TO MY FATHER.' signed 'E.B.B. LONDON, 50, WIMPOLE STREET, | 1844'; [v] 'PREFACE'; [xv] 'CONTENTS'; [1] fly title 'A DRAMA OF EXILE.'; [2] 'Persons of the Drama.'; [3] text; [120] blank; [121] fly title 'SONNETS.'; [122] blank; [123] 'THE SOUL'S EXPRESSION.'; 124 'THE SERAPH AND POET.'; 125 'ON A PORTRAIT OF WORDSWORTH, BY | R. B. HAYDON.'; 126 'PAST AND FUTURE.'; 127 'IRREPARABLENESS.'; 128 'TEARS.'; 129 'GRIEF.'; 130 'SUBSTITUTION.'; 131 'COMFORT.'; 132 'PERPLEXED MUSIC.'; 133 'WORK.'; 134 'FUTURITY.'; 135 'THE TWO SAYINGS.'; 136 'THE LOOK.'; 137 'THE MEANING OF THE LOOK.'; 138 'A THOUGHT FOR A LONELY DEATH-BED.'; 139 'WORK AND CONTEMPLATION.'; 140 'PAIN IN PLEASURE.'; 141 'AN APPREHENSION.'; 142 'DISCONTENT.'; 143 'PATIENCE TAUGHT BY NATURE.'; 144 'CHEERFULNESS TAUGHT BY REASON.'; 145 'EXAGGERATION.'; 146 'ADEQUACY.'; 147 'TO GEORGE SAND. | A DESIRE.'; 148 'TO GEORGE SAND. | A RECOGNITION.'; 149 'THE PRISONER.'; 150 'INSUFFICIENCY.'; [151] fly title 'THE | ROMAUNT OF THE PAGE.'; [152] blank; 153 text; [171] fly title 'THE LAY OF THE BROWN ROSARY.'; [172] blank; 173 text; 202 'THE MOURNFUL MOTHER, | (OF THE DEAD BLIND).'; 206 'A VALEDICTION.'; 209 'LADY GERALDINE'S COURTSHIP.'; 250 'END OF VOL. I.', printer's imprint; [251] advertisement for 'THE SERAPHIM, AND OTHER POEMS.'; [252] blank.

Vol. 2 [i] title page; [ii] printer's imprint; [iii] 'CONTENTS.'; [1] fly title 'A VISION OF POETS.'; [2] twelve line quotation from 'BRITANNIA'S PASTORALS.'; [3] text; [60] blank; [61] fly title 'RHYME OF THE DUCHESS MAY.'; [62] blank; [63] text; 96 'THE LADY'S YES.'; 98 'THE POET AND THE BIRD. | A FABLE.'; 100 'THE LOST BOWER.'; 123 'A CHILD ASLEEP.'; 127 'THE CRY OF THE CHILDREN.'; 136 'CROWNED AND WEDDED.'; 142 'CROWNED AND BURIED.'; 152 'TO FLUSH MY DOG.'; 159 'THE FOURFOLD ASPECT.'; 166 'A FLOWER IN A LETTER.'; 173 'THE CRY OF THE HUMAN.'; 180 'A LAY OF THE EARLY ROSE.'; 191 'BERTHA IN THE LANE.'; 203 'THAT DAY. | FOR MUSIC.'; 205 'LOVED ONCE.'; 209 'A

RHAPSODY OF LIFE'S PROGRESS.'; 219 'L.E.L.'s LAST QUESTION.'; 223 'THE HOUSE OF CLOUDS.'; 229 'CATARINA TO CAMOËNS.'; 237 'A PORTRAIT.'; 241 'SLEEPING AND WATCHING.'; 244 'WINE OF CYPRUS.'; 254 'THE ROMANCE OF THE SWAN'S NEST.'; 260 'LESSONS FROM THE GORSE.'; 262 'THE DEAD PAN.'; 275 'THE END.' [variant, see note below]; [276] printer's imprint.

Typography and paper: Vol. 1 $1,2(-B1) signed at center of foot. E2 signed E only. Running titles set in rom. caps. with the titles of the individual poems as 'A DRAMA OF EXILE.' Pagination set in the outer margin of the headline except pages 153, 173, 202, 206, 209 which are centered at the top. In the direction line on the first leaf of each gathering is printed 'VOL. I.' Text irregular, 22 lines + headline and direction line. Leaf H1^r type page measures 12.1 (13.2) × 7.5+ cm. Gutter margins measure, pp. 72–73 = 2.9 cm; 136–137 = 2.5 cm; 168–169 = 4.0 cm. White wove paper unwatermarked. Sheets bulk 1.7 cm. Vol. 2 $1,2 signed with the typographical features of Vol. 1. Pages 96, 98, 100, 127, 136, 142, 152, 159, 166, 173, 180, 191, 203, 205, 209, 219, 223, 229, 237, 241, 244, 254, 260, 262 centered at the top of the page. Gutter margins measure, pp. 72–73 = 2.4 cm; 136–137 = 2.4 cm; 152–153 = 3.9 cm. Sheets bulk 1.7 cm.

Binding: Slate green vertically ribbed (T) cloth. Sides blind stamped with two rules enclosing a floral pattern centered to an arabesque design. Spine: '[rule] | [thin and thick rule] | [thick and thin rule] | POEMS | BY | E. B. BARRETT | [thin and thick rule] | [thick and thin rule] | VOL. I. [II.] | [thin and thick rule] | [thick and thin rule] | [rule] | [rule]'. All rules stamped in blind; all lettering in gilt. Yellow coated end papers. In some copies a publisher's catalogue of 8 pages is inserted at the front of volume one. Five stab holes at inner margin. Top and fore edges unopened; bottom edge untrimmed.

Binding variant: Slate green vertically ribbed (T) cloth. Sides blind stamped with a single rule enclosing a simple floral design. Stamping on spine as above. Wove white end papers, also cream coated end papers.

Notes: Published on August 14, 1844, at twelve shillings. According to Wise the edition consisted of 1,500 copies. Publisher's catalogues inserted in the front of volume one have been seen with the following dates: June 1, 1844; August 1, 1844; October 1, 1844; January 1, 1845; August 1, 1845; July 1, 1846. These of course bear no relation to the priority of the printings and I have seen a first impression with an August 1 catalogue and a second impression with a June 1 catalogue (TxU). Presentation copies of the later impressions signed by E.B.B. and dated August 1844 suggests all impressions were struck off before the day of publication.

First Impression

As above with the following points: Vol. 1 Page [1] measures 8.0 cm. from direction line to the fly title. Lines 11–12 page 141 read ". . . let the flood/ Of your salt scorn dash on me!" (TxU Aitken) Vol. 2 Pages 160, 163 correctly numbered. Page 275 is without the words 'THE END.' (TxU Hanley 1)

Second Impression

As above with these points: Vol. 1 page [1] measures 7.7+ cm. from the direction line to the fly title. Lines 11–12 page 141 read ". . . Let your flood/ Of bitter scorn dash on me!" (TxU Hanley 1) Vol. 2 Page 160 misnumbered 60; page 163 correctly numbered. Page 275 has the words 'THE END.' (UI)

Third Impression

As above with these points: Vol. 1 page [1] measures 7.5 cm. from the direction line to the fly title. Lines 11–12 revised as in second impression. (TxWB) Vol. 2 Page 160 correctly numbered. Page 163 misnumbered 16; page 275 has the words 'THE END.' (TxWB)
Note: not only do copies exist containing mixed sheets of each impression, but also most "sets" are made up of volumes from the different impressions.

Copies examined: MH MB MWelC CtY NN DLC ICN IU TxWB TxU CSMH CLU–C L O.

A5a : A Drama of Exile 1844

[*within a ruled frame and corner ornaments*] A | DRAMA OF EXILE: | AND | OTHER POEMS. | BY | ELIZABETH BAR-RETT BARRETT, | AUTHOR OF 'THE SERAPHIM: AND OTHER POEMS.' | VOL. I. [II.] | NEW-YORK: | HENRY G. LANGLEY, | NO. 8, ASTOR-HOUSE. | [*short rule 0.3 cm.*] | M.DCCC.XLV.

Special imprints: Vol. 1 (on p. [ii] at the foot) H. LUDWIG, PRINTER, | Nos. 70 and 72, Vesey-st. Vol. 2 (on p. [ii] as above.)

Collation: Vol. 1 17.7 × 11.3 cm; 1⁶ 2–11¹² 12⁶; 132 leaves. Vol. 2 17.7 × 11.3 cm; [13]² 14–24¹² 25¹⁰; 144 leaves.

Pagination: Vol. 1 [i–iii] iv [v] vi–x [xi] xii, [13–15] 16–131 [132–135] 136–162 [163–165] 166–182 [183–185] 186–213 [214] 215–217 [218] 219–220 [221–223] 224–264. Vol. 2 [i–iii] iv, [5–7] 8–63 [64–67] 68–99 [100] 101 [102] 103 [104] 105–126 [127] 128–130 [131] 132–139 [140] 141–145 [146] 147–155 [156] 157–162 [163] 164–169 [170] 171–176 [177] 178–183 [184] 185–194 [195] 196–206 [207] 208 [209] 210–212 [213] 214–222 [223] 224–226 [227] 228–232 [233] 234–240 [241] 242–244 [245] 246–247 [248] 249–257 [258] 259–263 [264] 265 [266] 267–279 [280]. [1] 2–8.

Contents: Vol. 1 [i] title page; [ii] printer's imprint; [iii] 'DEDI-CATION. | [*wavy rule*] | TO MY FATHER.'; [v] 'PREFACE | TO THE | AMERICAN EDITION.'; [xi] 'CONTENTS.'; [13] fly title 'A DRAMA OF EXILE.'; [14] '𝔓𝔢𝔯𝔰𝔬𝔫𝔰 𝔬𝔣 𝔱𝔥𝔢 𝔇𝔯𝔞𝔪𝔞.'; [15] text; [132] blank; [133] fly title 'SONNETS.'; [134] blank; [135] 'SONNETS. | [*wavy rule*] | THE SOUL'S EXPRESSION.'; 136 'THE SERAPH AND POET.'; 137 'ON A PORTRAIT OF WORDSWORTH, BY | B. R. HAYDON.'; 138 'PAST AND FU-TURE.'; 139 'IRREPARABLENESS'; 140 'TEARS.'; 141 'GRIEF.'; 142 'SUBSTITUTION.'; 143 'COMFORT.'; 144 'PERPLEXED MUSIC.'; 145 'WORK.'; 146 'FUTURITY.'; 147 'THE TWO SAY-INGS.'; 148 'THE LOOK.'; 149 'THE MEANING OF THE LOOK.'; 150 'A THOUGHT FOR A LONELY DEATH-BED.'; 151 'WORK AND CONTEMPLATION.'; 152 'PAIN AND PLEASURE.'; 153 'AN APPREHENSION.'; 154 'DISCON-TENT.'; 155 'PATIENCE TAUGHT BY NATURE.'; 156 'CHEERFULNESS TAUGHT BY REASON.'; 157 'EXAGGERA-TION.'; 158 'ADEQUACY.'; 159 'TO GEORGE SAND. | [*rule*] | A DESIRE.'; 160 'TO GEORGE SAND. | [*rule*] | A RECOG-NITION.'; 161 'THE PRISONER.'; 162 'INSUFFICIENCY.'; [163] fly title 'THE | ROMAUNT OF THE PAGE.'; [164] blank; [165] text; [183] fly title 'THE | LAY OF THE BROWN ROSARY.'; [184] blank; [185] text; [214] 'THE MOURNFUL MOTHER, | (OF THE DEAD BLIND.)'; [218] 'A VALEDIC-TION.'; [221] fly title 'LADY GERALDINE'S COURTSHIP. | A ROMANCE OF THE AGE.'; [222] blank; [223] text. 264 'END OF VOL. I.'

Vol. 2 [i] title page; [ii] printer's imprint; [iii] contents; [5] fly title 'A VISION OF POETS.'; [6] twelve line quotation from 'BRI-TANNIA'S PASTORALS.'; [7] text; [64] blank; 65 fly title 'RHYME OF THE DUCHESS MAY.'; [66] blank; [67] text; [100] 'THE LADY'S YES.'; [102] 'THE POET AND THE BIRD. | A FABLE.'; [104] 'THE LOST BOWER.'; [127] 'A CHILD ASLEEP.'; [131] 'THE CRY OF THE CHILDREN.'; [140] 'CROWNED AND WEDDED.'; [146] 'CROWNED AND BUR-

IED.'; [156] 'TO FLUSH, MY DOG.'; [163] 'THE FOURFOLD
ASPECT.'; [170] 'A FLOWER IN A LETTER. | WRITTEN
1839.'; [177] 'THE CRY OF THE HUMAN.'; [184] 'A LAY OF
THE EARLY ROSE.'; [195] 'BERTHA IN THE LANE.'; [207]
'THAT DAY. | FOR MUSIC.'; [209] 'LOVED ONCE.'; [213] 'A
RHAPSODY OF LIFE'S PROGRESS.'; [223] 'L.E.L.'S LAST
QUESTION.'; [227] 'THE HOUSE OF CLOUDS.'; [233] 'CATA-
RINA TO CAMOËNS.'; [241] 'A PORTRAIT.'; [245] 'SLEEP-
ING AND WATCHING.'; [248] 'WINE OF CYPRUS.'; [258]
'THE ROMANCE OF THE SWAN'S NEST.'; [264] 'LESSONS
FROM THE GORSE.'; [266] 'THE DEAD PAN.'; [279] 'END
OF THE SECOND VOLUME.'; [280] blank; [1] 2–8 publisher's
catalogue of 8 pages advertising 'VALUABLE WORKS | PUB-
LISHED BY | HENRY G. LANGLEY, | 8 ASTOR HOUSE, |
NEW YORK.'

Typography and paper: Vol. 1 $1,5* signed below ruled frame to-
ward inner margin of foot. Leaf 1₃ signed 1*; leaf 12₃ signed 12*.
Each page enclosed by a ruled frame with rosettes as corner ornaments. Running titles set within ruled frame above a single rule in
rom. caps with the titles of the individual poems as 'THE ROM-
AUNT OF THE PAGE.' Pagination set in the outer margin of the
headline. Text irregular, 22 lines + headline and direction line.
Leaf 5₅ᵣ measures 11.9 (14.5) × 8.1 cm. Gutter margins measure,
pp. 96–97 = 3.2 cm; 120–121 = 3.0 cm; 216–217 = 3.0 cm. Page 137
has no ornament in the lower right hand corner in all copies seen.
Page 145 has no period following the word 'SONNETS' in the
headlines. White wove paper unwatermarked. Sheets bulk 2.1 cm.
Vol. 2 $1,5* signed with the typographical features of Vol. 1. Sigs
19–23 are printed on a heavier, whiter paper than the rest of the
book. Leaf 21₅ missigned 20*. Gutter margins measure, pp. 112–
113 = 3.2 cm; 136–137 = 3.0 cm; 232–[233] = 3.1 cm. Sheets bulk
2.3 cm.

Notes: Published October 1, 1844 at $1.00; 1500 copies were
printed in the edition. In a letter to her sister Elizabeth remarks
that her American publisher would use only the finest types and
highest quality of paper.

Binding: Yellow paper covered boards: Printed paper label on
spine: '[*double rule*] | DRAMA | OF | EXILE, | AND | OTHER
POEMS. | BY | E. B. BARRETT. | TWO VOLS. | [*short rule*] |
VOL. I. [II.] | [*double rule*]' White wove end papers. Single bind-
er's leaf at front and back. Five stab holes at inner margin. All
edges trimmed. (CtY)

Binding variants: Claret vertically ribbed (T) cloth. Sides blind stamped with a frame of three rules with floral corner points enclosing a wreath of leaves and an eight pointed floral design. Spine: '[*ornamental design of two bell shaped flowers*] | DRAMA | OF | EXILE | AND | OTHER POEMS | [*short rule*] | BARRETT. | [*short rule*] | VOL. 1 [2] | [*design of two bell shaped flowers as above and two floral ornaments of three parts each*]' All in gilt. Yellow end papers. (CtY)

Green vertically ribbed (T) cloth. Sides blind stamped with a frame of three rules enclosing a lyre. Spine: '[*two stems of flowers surrounding a fan shaped design*] | DRAMA | OF | EXILE | AND | OTHER POEMS | [*short rule*] | BARRETT. | [*short rule*] | VOL. 1 [2] | [*ornamental floral design*]' All in gilt. (MH)

Also in purple diaper cloth with the same stamping. (MB)

Brown vertically ribbed (T) cloth. Sides blind stamped with a frame of three rules. Running around the edge is an ornate design of leaves enclosing a crest with seven plumes. Spine: '[*floral device surrounding a group of seven circles*] | DRAMA | OF | EXILE | AND | OTHER POEMS | [*short rule*] | BARRETT. | [*short rule*] | VOL. 1 [2] | [*bouquet of flowers flanked on each side by two vertical rules and on top and bottom by a group of seven circles with floral ornamentation*]' All in gilt. (TxWB)

Olive green vertically ribbed (T) cloth. Sides blind stamped with a frame of three rules with floral corner points enclosing a center design of two groups of leaves and four flower stems each decorated to a spiral. Spine: '[*ornamental floral design*] | DREAM | OF | EXILE | AND | OTHER POEMS | [*short rule*] | BARRETT. | [*short rule*] | VOL. 1 [2] | [*two floral designs facing each other, flanked on each side by semi-circles of fifteen dots*]' All in gilt. (CtY)

Brown vertically ribbed (T) cloth. Sides blind stamped with a frame of three rules. Running around the edge is an ornate floral design enclosing a centerpiece of leaves and flower petals. Spine: '[*floral design of two large flower heads and intertwining stems*] | DRAMA | OF | EXILE | AND | OTHER POEMS | [*short rule*] | BARRETT. | [*short rule*] | VOL. 1 [2] | [*design of flower heads as above and crown shaped design with floral ornamentation*]' All in gilt. (CtY)

Claret vertically ribbed (T) cloth. Sides blind stamped with a frame of three rules with floral corner points enclosing a hexagon shaped design. Spine: '[*floral ornament of three parts*] | DRAMA | OF | EXILE | AND | OTHER POEMS | [*short rule*] | BARRETT. | [*short rule*] | VOL. 1 [2] | [*ornament as above repeated three times*]' All in gilt. (TxWB)

Impressions

There are at least two impressions of this book with variants in the following apparent order:

A. Vol. 1 Page 65 is numbered correctly. Page 70 has the ornament present in the upper left hand corner. Page 91 is numbered correctly. Page 137 has the ornament present in the upper left hand corner. Page 162 has the ornament present in the upper left hand corner. Page 174 has the ornament present in the upper left hand corner. Line 19, page 180 reads "And see if ye can find him!" Page 210 has the ornament present in the upper left hand corner.

Vol. 2 Page 218 is numbered correctly. Page 223 the title reads "... QUESTION." Page 244 is numbered correctly.

B. Vol. 1 Page 65 unnumbered. Page 70 has no ornament in the upper left hand corner. Page 91 is unnumbered. Page 137 has no ornament in the upper left hand corner. Page 162 has no ornament in the upper left hand corner. Page 174 has no ornament in the upper left hand corner. Line 19, page 180 reads "And see if. ye can find im!" Page 210 has no ornament in the upper left hand corner.

Vol. 2 Page 218 misnumbered 18. Page 223 reads ". . . QUESTIO ." Page 244 misnumbered 2 . Copies containing mixed sheets can occur in 256 possible combinations for Vol. 1; 8 for Vol. 2 and I have never found any two copies alike. Several variations seen are as follows:

Vol. 1 p. 65 numbered correctly; p. 70 ornament absent; p. 91 unnumbered; p. 137 ornament present; p. 162 ornament absent; p. 174 ornament absent; p. 180.19 reads "And see if ye can find im!"; p. 210 ornament present. Vol. 2 p. 218 misnumbered 18; p. 223 reads "... QUESTIO ."; p. 244 numbered correctly. (TxWB)

Vol. 1 p. 65 numbered correctly; p. 70 ornament present; p. 91 numbered correctly; p. 137 ornament absent; p. 162 ornament present; p. 174 ornament present; p. 180.19 reads "And see if ye can find him!"; p. 210 ornament absent. Vol. 2 p. 218 numbered correctly; p. 223 reads ". . . QUESTION."; p. 244 numbered correctly. (TxWB)

Vol. 1 p. 65 unnumbered; p. 70 ornament present; p. 91 unnumbered; p. 137 ornament present; p. 162 ornament absent; p. 174 ornament absent; p. 180.19 reads "And see if ye can find im!"; p. 210 ornament absent; Vol. 2 p. 218 misnumbered 18; p. 223 reads "... QUESTION."; p. 244 numbered correctly. (MB)

Vol. 1 p. 65 numbered correctly; p. 70 ornament present; p. 91 unnumbered; p. 137 ornament absent; p. 162 ornament present; p.

174 ornament present; p. 180.19 reads "And see if ye can find him!"; p. 210 ornament present. Vol. 2 p. 218 numbered correctly; p. 223 reads ". . . QUESTIO ."; p. 244 misnumbered 2 (CSmH)

Copies examined: NN MH MWelC MB CtY DLC TxWB WB L CSmH.

A6 : Poems 1850

POEMS. | BY | ELIZABETH BARRETT BROWNING. | NEW EDITION. | IN TWO VOLUMES. | VOL. I. [II.] | LONDON: | CHAPMAN & HALL, 193, PICCADILLY. | (Late 186, STRAND.) | 1850.

Special imprints: Vol. 1 (p. [iv] and p. [363] in the center) LONDON: | BRADBURY AND EVANS, PRINTERS, WHITE-FRIARS. Vol. 2 (p. [iv] at the center and p. 480 at the foot), imprint as above.

Collation: Vol. 1 17.1 × 10.5 cm; [a]⁴ b² B–Z⁸ AA⁶; 188 leaves. Vol. 2 [A]⁴ B–HH⁸; 244 leaves.

Pagination: Vol. 1 [i–v] vi [vii] viii [ix] x–xii, [1–3] 4–91 [92–95] 96–107 [108] 109–136 [137–139] 140–190 [191–193] 194–198 [199–201] 202–249 [250–253] 254–276 [277–279] 280–289 [290–293] 294–314 [315–316] 319 = 317 318–362 [363–364]. Vol. 2 [i–v] vi–viii, [1] 2–16 [17] 18–38 [39] 40–48 [49] 50–79 [80] 81–84 [85] 86–96 [97] 98–128 [129] 130–141 [142] 143–149 [150] 151–153 [154] 155–159 [160] 161–164 [165] 166–173 [174] 175–181 [182] 183–189 [190] 191–198 [199] 200–201 [202] 203 [204] 205 [206] 207–208 [209] 210–211 [212] 213–215 [216] 217–220 [221] 222–229 [230] 231–235 [236] 237–255 [256] 257–260 [261] 262–264 [265] 266–269 [270] 271–272 [273] 274–275 [276] 277–283 [284] 285–291 [292] 293–300 [301] 302 [303] 304–308 [309] 310–311 [312] 313–316 [317] 318–319 [320] 321–324 [325] 326–328 [329] 330–334 [335] 336–337 [338] 339–342 [343] 344–346 [347] 348–349 [350] 351–352 [353] 354 [355] 356 [357–361] 362 [363] 364 [365] 366–367 [368] 369 [370] 371–374 [375] 376–380 [381] 382 [383] 384–386 [387] 388–390 [391] 392–393 [394] 395 [396] 397 [398] 399 [400] 401–402 [403] 404 [405] 406 [407] 408 [409–410] 411–423 [424] 425–430 [431] 432–437 [438] 439–480.

Contents: Vol. 1 [i] half title 'POEMS.'; [ii] blank; [iii] title page; [iv] printer's imprint; [v] 'DEDICATION. | [*french rule*] | TO

MY FATHER.'; [vii] 'ADVERTISEMENT.' signed FLORENCE,
| January, 1850.'; [ix] 'CONTENTS.'; [1] fly title 'A DRAMA OF
EXILE.'; [2] blank; [3] text; [92] blank; [93] fly title 'THE SERA-
PHIM. | "I look for Angels' songs, and hear Him cry." | GILES
FLETCHER.'; [94] blank; [95] 'THE SERAPHIM. | [french
rule] | PART THE FIRST.'; [108] 'PART THE SECOND.';
134 'THE EPILOGUE.'; [137] fly title 'PROMETHEUS
BOUND.'; [138] blank; [139] text; [191] fly title 'A LAMENT
FOR ADONIS. | FROM THE GREEK OF BION.'; [192] blank;
[193] text; [199] fly title 'A VISION OF POETS.'; [200] twelve
line quotation from 'BRITANNIA'S PASTORALS.'; [201] text;
[250] blank; [251] fly title 'THE POET'S VOW. | — O be wiser
thou, | Instructed that true knowledge leads to love. | WORDS-
WORTH.'; [252] blank; [253] 'THE POET'S VOW. | [french
rule] | PART THE FIRST.'; 259 'PART THE SECOND.'; 265
'PART THE THIRD.'; 267 'PART THE FOURTH.'; 271 'PART
THE FIFTH.'; [277] fly title "THE ROMAUNT OF MARGRET
| Can my affections find out nothing best, | But still and still re-
move? — | QUARLES.'; [278] blank; [279] text; [290] blank;
[291] fly title 'ISOBEL'S CHILD. | — so find we profit, By losing
of our prayers. | SHAKESPEARE.'; [292] blank; [293] text; [315]
fly title 'SONNETS.'; [316] blank; 319 = 317 'THE SOUL'S EX-
PRESSION.'; 318 'THE SERAPH AND POET.'; 319 'BEREAV-
MENT.'; 320 'CONSOLATION.'; 321 'TO MARY RUSSELL
MITFORD | IN HER GARDEN.'; 322 'ON A PORTRAIT OF
WORDSWORTH BY | R. B. HAYDON.'; 323 'PAST AND FU-
TURE.'; 324 'IRREPARABLENESS.'; 325 'TEARS.'; 326 'GRIEF.';
327 'SUBSTITUTION.'; 328 'COMFORT.'; 329 'PERPLEXED
MUSIC.' | AFFECTIONATELY INSCRIBED TO E. J.'; 330
'WORK.'; 331 'FUTURITY.'; 332 'THE TWO SAYINGS.'; 333
'THE LOOK.'; 334 'THE MEANING OF THE LOOK.'; 335 'A
THOUGHT FOR A LONELY DEATHBED. | INSCRIBED TO
MY FRIEND E.C.'; 336 'WORK AND CONTEMPLATION.'; 337
'PAIN IN PLEASURE.'; 338 'FLUSH OR FAUNUS.'; 339 'FI-
NITE AND INFINITE.'; 340 'AN APPREHENSION.'; 341 'DIS-
CONTENT.'; 342 'PATIENCE TAUGHT BY NATURE.'; 343
'CHEERFULNESS TAUGHT BY REASON.'; 344 'EXAGGERA-
TION.'; 345 'ADEQUACY.'; 346 'TO GEORGE SAND. | A DE-
SIRE.'; 347 'TO GEORGE SAND. | A RECOGNITION.'; 348
'THE PRISONER.'; 349 'INSUFFICIENCY.'; 350 'TWO
SKETCHES | I'; 351 'II.'; 352 'MOUNTAINEER AND POET.';
353 'THE POET.'; 354 'HIRAM POWERS'S GREEK SLAVE.';
355 'LIFE.'; 356 'LOVE.'; 357 'HEAVEN AND EARTH.'; 358
'THE PROSPECT.'; 359 'HUGH STUART BOYD. | HIS BLIND-
NESS.'; 360 'HUGH STUART BOYD. | HIS DEATH, 1848.'; 361

'HUGH STUART BOYD. | LEGACIES.'; 362 'FUTURE AND PAST.'; [363] printer's imprint; [364] blank.

Vol. 2 [i] half title 'POEMS.'; [ii] blank; [iii] title page; [iv] printer's imprint; [v] 'CONTENTS.'; [1] POEMS | [*french rule*] | 'THE ROMAUNT OF THE PAGE.'; [17] 'THE LAY OF THE BROWN ROSARY.'; [39] 'A ROMANCE OF THE GANGES.'; [49] 'RHYME OF THE DUCHESS MAY.'; [80] 'THE RO-MANCE OF THE SWAN'S NEST.'; [85] 'BERTHA IN THE LANE.'; [97] 'LADY GERALDINE'S COURTSHIP. | A RO-MANCE OF THE AGE.'; [129] 'THE | RUNAWAY SLAVE AT PILGRIM'S POINT.'; [142] 'THE CRY OF THE CHILDREN.'; [150] 'A CHILD ASLEEP.'; [154] 'THE FOURFOLD ASPECT.'; [160] 'NIGHT AND THE MERRY MAN.'; [165] 'EARTH AND HER PRAISERS.'; [174] 'THE VIRGIN MARY TO THE CHILD JESUS.'; [182] 'AN ISLAND.'; [190] 'THE SOUL'S TRAVEL-LING.'; [199] 'TO BETTINE, THE CHILD-FRIEND OF GOETHE.'; [202] 'MAN AND NATURE.'; [204] 'A SEA-SIDE WALK.'; [206] 'THE SEA-MEW. | AFFECTIONATELY IN-SCRIBED TO M.E.H.'; [209] ''FELICIA HEMANS. | TO L.E.L., REFERRING TO HER MONODY ON THAT POETESS.'; [212] 'L.E.L.'S LAST QUESTION.'; [216] 'CROWNED AND WEDDED.'; [221] 'CROWNED AND BURIED.'; [230] 'TO FLUSH, MY DOG.'; [236] 'THE LOST BOWER.'; [256] 'THE DESERTED GARDEN.'; [261] 'MY DOVES.'; [265] 'HECTOR IN THE GARDEN.'; [270] 'SLEEPING AND WATCHING.'; [273] 'A SONG AGAINST SINGING. | TO E.J.H.'; [276] 'WINE OF CYPRUS.'; [284] 'A RHAPSODY OF LIFE'S PROGRESS.'; [292] 'A LAY OF THE EARLY ROSE.'; [301] 'THE POET AND THE BIRD. | A FABLE.'; [303] 'THE CRY OF THE HUMAN.'; [309] 'A PORTRAIT.'; [312] 'CONFESSIONS.'; [317] 'LOVED ONCE.'; [320] 'THE HOUSE OF CLOUDS.'; [325] 'A SAB-BATH MORNING AT SEA.'; [329] 'A FLOWER IN A LET-TER.'; [335] 'THE MASK.'; [338] 'CALLS ON THE HEART.'; [343] 'WISDOM UNAPPLIED.'; [347] 'MEMORY AND HOPE.'; [350] 'HUMAN LIFE'S MYSTERY.'; [353] 'A CHILD'S THOUGHT OF GOD.'; [355] 'THE CLAIM.'; [357] 'LIFE AND LOVE.'; [358] 'INCLUSIONS.'; [359] 'INSUFFICIENCY.'; [360] 'SONG OF THE ROSE. | ATTRIBUTED TO SAPPHO.'; [361] 'A DEAD ROSE.'; [363] 'THE EXILE'S RETURN.'; [365] 'THE SLEEP.'; [368] 'THE MEASURE.'; [370] 'COWPER'S GRAVE.'; [375] 'SOUNDS.'; [381] 'THE WEAKEST THING.'; [383] 'THE PET-NAME.'; [387] 'THE MOURNING MOTHER | (OF THE DEAD BLIND).'; [391] 'A VALEDICTION.'; [394] 'LESSONS FROM THE GORSE.'; [396] 'THE LADY'S YES.'

[398] 'A WOMAN'S SHORTCOMINGS.'; [400] 'A MAN'S RE-
QUIREMENTS.'; [403] 'A YEAR'S SPINNING.'; [405]
'CHANGE UPON CHANGE.'; [407] 'THAT DAY.'; [409] 'A
REED.'; [410] 'THE DEAD PAN.'; [424] 'A CHILD'S GRAVE
AT FLORENCE. | [french rule] | A.A.E.C. | BORN JULY, 1848.
DIED NOVEMBER, 1849.'; [431] 'CATARINA TO CAMOENS.';
[438] 'SONNETS FROM THE PORTUGUESE. | I. | I
THOUGHT once how Theocritus had sung.'; 439 'II. | BUT only
three in all God's universe.'; 440 'III. | UNLIKE are we, unlike, O
princely Heart!'; 441 'IV. | THOU hast thy calling to some palace
floor,'; 442 'V. | I LIFT my heavy heart up solemnly,'; 443 'VI. | GO
from me. Yet I feel that I shall stand'; 444 'VII. | THE face of all
the world is changed, I think,'; 445 'VIII. | WHAT can I give thee
back, O liberal'; 446 'IX. | CAN it be right to give what I can
give?'; 447 'X. | YET love, mere love, is beautiful indeed'; 448 'XI. |
AND therefore if to love can be desert,'; 449 'XII. | INDEED this
very love which is my boast.'; 450 'XIII. | AND wilt thou have me
fashion into speech'; 451 'XIV. | IF thou must love me, let it be for
nought'; 452 'XV. | ACCUSE me not, beseech thee, that I wear';
453 'XVI. | AND yet, because thou overcomst so,'; 454 'XVII. | MY
poet, thou canst touch on all the notes'; 455 'XVIII. | I NEVER
gave a lock of my hair away'; 456 'XIX. | THE soul's Rialto hath its
merchandise;'; 457 'XX. | BELOVED, my Beloved, when I think';
458 'XXI. | SAY over again and yet once over again'; 459 'XXII. |
WHEN our two souls stand up erect and strong,'; 460 'XXIII. | IS
it indeed so? If I lay here dead,'; 461 'XXIV. | LET the world's
sharpness like a clasping knife'; 462 'XXV. | A HEAVY heart, Be-
loved, have I borne'; 463 'XXVI. | I LIVED with visions for my
company'; 464 'XXVII. | MY own Beloved, who hast lifted me'; 465
'XXVIII. | MY letters! all dead paper, . . mute and white! — '; 466
'XXIX. | I THINK of thee! — my thoughts do twine and bud'; 467
'XXX. | I SEE thine image through my tears tonight,'; 468 'XXXI. |
THOU comest! all is said without a word.'; 469 'XXXII. | THE first
time that the sun rose on thine oath'; 470 'XXXIII. | YES, call me
by my pet-name! let me hear'; 471 'XXXIV. | WITH the same
heart, I said, I'll answer thee'; 472 'XXXV. | IF I leave all for thee,
wilt thou exchange'; 473 'XXXVI. | WHEN we met first and loved,
I did not build'; 474 'XXXVII. | PARDON, oh, pardon, that my
soul should make'; 475 'XXXVIII. | FIRST time he kissed me, he
but only kissed'; 476 'XXXIX. | BECAUSE thou hast the power
and own'st the grace'; 477 'XL. | OH, yes! they love through all
this world of ours!'; 478 'XLI. | I THANK all who have loved me in
their hearts,'; 479 'XLII. | HOW do I love thee? Let me count the
ways.'; 480 'XLIII. | BELOVED, thou hast brought me many
flowers,' 'END OF VOL. II.', printer's imprint.

Typography and paper: Vol. 1 $1,2 signed toward outer margin of foot. Running titles set in rom. caps. with the titles of the individual poems as 'A ROMANCE OF THE GANGES.'; Pagination set in the outer margin of the headline. In the direction line on the first leaf of each gathering is printed 'VOL. I.' Text irregular, 29 lines + headline and direction line. Leaf 12ʳ measures 12.3 (13.3) × 7.6 cm. Gutter margins measure, pp. 152–153 = 3.1 cm; 216–217 = 4.4 cm; 296–297 = 3.9 cm. Page 317 misnumbered 319. White wove paper unwatermarked. Sheets bulk 2.5 cm.
Vol. 2 $1,2 signed with the typographical features of Vol. 1. Gutter margins measure, pp. 136–137 = 3.2 cm; 200–201 = 4.2 cm; 376–377 = 3.8 cm. Sheets bulk 3.2 cm.

Binding: Blue vertically ribbed (T) cloth. Sides blind stamped with a floral border enclosing a centered arabesque. Spine: '[*conventional decorated band*] | ELIZᴴ BARRETT | BROWNING's POEMS | [*short rule*] | VOL. I. [II.] | LONDON | CHAPMAN & HALL | [*conventional decorated band*]'. Bands at head and foot of spine stamped in blind; all lettering in gilt. Yellow coated end papers. Five stab hole at inner margin. Binder's stamp on paste down at back reads 'BOUND BY T. R. EELES & SON CURSITOR ST. LONDON.' Top and fore edges unopened; bottom edge untrimmed. This same binding was used also for E.B.B.'s *Casa Guidi Windows* and R. B.'s Poems, 1850.

Notes: Published November 1, 1850 at sixteen shillings. Copy for this edition with ms. corrections made by E.B.B. is at Wellesley.

First state

As described with this variant: Publisher's imprint at the foot of the title page reads 'CHAPMAN & HALL, 186, STRAND.' *Not seen*. description furnished from photocopy provided by the Lilly Library, Bloomington, Indiana.

Second state

As described with the publisher's imprint at the foot of the title page reading 'CHAPMAN & HALL, 193 PICCADILLY | (LATE 186 STRAND.)' The first state of the book must be extremely rare, for as late as 1963 only 3 copies were located, and none were present in any library I visited. There is no evidence that the book was actually "issued" after its publication in the two forms described and the scarcity of copies suggests that the title page was reset prior to publication. One copy is at The Cambridge University Library.

Copies examined: MWelC TxWB TxU IU L O.

A7 : Casa Guidi Windows 1851

CASA GUIDI WINDOWS. | A Poem. | BY | ELIZABETH BAR-
RETT BROWNING. | LONDON: | CHAPMAN & HALL, 193,
PICCADILLY. | 1851.

Special imprints: (p. [iv] at the center) LONDON: | BRAD-
BURY AND EVANS, PRINTERS, WHITEFRIARS. (p. 140 at
the foot) imprint as above.

Collation: 17.1 × 10.6 cm; [a]² b² B–I⁸ K⁶; 74 leaves.

Pagination: [i–v] vi–vii [viii], [1] 2–137 [138] 139–140.

Contents: [i] half title 'CASA GUIDI WINDOWS.'; [ii] blank;
[iii] title page; [iv] printer's imprint; [v] 'ADVERTISEMENT.'
dated 'FLORENCE, 1851.' [viii] blank; [1] CASA GUIDI WIN-
DOWS. | [*double rule*] | PART I.'; 84 'PART II.'; [138] 'NOTES.';
140 printer's imprint.

Typography and paper: $1,2 signed toward outer margin of the
foot. Running titles set in rom. caps. as 'CASA GUIDI WIN-
DOWS.' Pagination set in outer margin of the headline. Text irregular, 16 lines + headline and direction line. Leaf H2ʳ type page
measures 11.8 (13.2) × 7.7 cm. Gutter margins measure pp. 24–
25 = 2.9 cm; 72–73 = 2.8 cm; 88–89 = 2.5 cm. White wove paper
unwatermarked. Sheets bulk 1.0 cm.

Binding: Blue vertically ribbed (T) cloth. Sides blind stamped
with floral border enclosing a centered arabesque. Spine: '[*con-
ventional decorated band*] | CASA GUIDI | WINDOWS | [*rule*] |
E. B. BROWNING | CHAPMAN & HALL | [*conventional dec-
orated band*]'. Bands at head and foot of spine stamped in blind;
all lettering in gilt. Yellow coated end papers. Five stab holes at
inner margin. Top and fore edges unopened; bottom edge untrimmed. In some copies a publisher's catalogue of 34 pages dated
1851 is inserted at back.

Binding variant: As above except at foot of spine above publisher's
imprint is gilt stamped 'LONDON'. (OB)

Notes: Published May 31, 1851 at five shillings. A manuscript (first
draft) is at Harvard.

First Impression
As described with the following points. On the title page the distance from 'CASA GUIDI WINDOWS' to 1851, measures 11.7 +
cm. The overall measurement of type page 88 is 11.7 cm. On page
133 the RT is normally set. (CLU–C copy 2)

Second Impression

As described with the following points. On the title page the distance from 'CASA GUIDI WINDOWS' to '1851' measures 11.5 cm. On page 88 an extra lead has been inserted at the end of stanza IV and the overall measurement of the type page is 11.8 cm. On page 133 the final letter 'I' in the word 'GUIDI' of the RT is separated from the other letters. (CLU–C copy 1)

Copies examined: MH MB MWelC NN CtY IU IaU ICN ICU DLC TxU TxWB CLU–C CSMH L O OB.

A8 : **Poems Third Edition** 1853

POEMS. | BY | ELIZABETH BARRETT BROWNING. | THIRD EDITION. | IN TWO VOLUMES. | VOL. I. [II.] | LONDON: | CHAPMAN & HALL, 193, PICCADILLY. | 1853.

Special imprints: Vol. 1 (p. [iv] and p. [363] at the center) LONDON: | BRADBURY AND EVANS, PRINTERS, WHITEFRIARS. Vol. 2 p. [iv] at the center and p. 480 at the foot, imprint as above.

Collation: Vol. 1. 17.1 × 10.6 cm; [a]⁴ b² B-Z⁸ AA⁶; 188 leaves. Vol. 2 17.1 × 10.6 cm; [A]⁴ B-HH⁸; 244 leaves.

Pagination: Vol. 1 [i–v] vi [vii] viii [ix] x–xii, [1–3] 4–92 [93–95] 96–106 [107] 108–135 [136–139] 140–190 [191–193] 194–198 [199–201] 202–249 [250–253] 254–276 [277–279] 280–289 [290–293] 294–314 [315–316] 317–362 [363–364]. Vol. 2 [i–v] vi–viii, [1] 2–16 [17] 18–38 [39] 40–48 [49] 50–79 [80] 81–84 [85] 86–96 [97] 98–128 [129] 130–141 [142] 143–149 [150] 151–153 [154] 155–159 [160] 161–164 [165] 166–173 [174] 175–181 [182] 183–189 [190] 191–198 [199] 200–201 [202] 203 [204] 205 [206] 207–208 [209] 210–211 [212] 213–215 [216] 217–220 [221] 222–229 [230] 231–235 [236] 237–255 [256] 257–260 [261]262–264 [265] 266–269 [270] 271–272 [273] 274–275 [276] 277–283 [284] 285–291 [292] 293–300 [301] 302 [303] 304–308 [309] 310–311 [312] 313–316 [317] 318–319 [320] 321–324 [325] 326–328 [329] 330–334 [335] 336–337 [338] 339–342 [343] 344–346 [347] 348–349 [350] 351–352 [353] 354 [355] 356 [357–361] 362 [363] 364 [365] 366–367 [368] 369 [370] 371–374 [375] 376–380 [381] 382 [383] 384–386 [387] 388–390 [391] 392–393 [394] 395 [396] 397 [398] 399 [400] 401–402 [403] 404 [405] 406 [407] 408 [409–410] 411–423 [424] 425–430 [431] 432–437 [438] 439–480.

Contents: Vol. 1. [i] half title 'POEMS.'; [ii] blank; [iii] title page [iv] printer's imprint; [v] '𝕯𝖊𝖉𝖎𝖈𝖆𝖙𝖎𝖔𝖓.' | [*french rule*] | 'TO

MY FATHER'; [vii] 'ADVERTISEMENT TO THE SECOND |
EDITION.'; viii 'POSTSCRIPT.' signed 'FLORENCE, 1853.'; [ix]
'CONTENTS.'; [1] fly title 'A DRAMA OF EXILE.'; [2] blank; [3]
text; [93] fly title 'THE SERAPHIM. | I look for Angels' songs and
hear Him cry. | GILES FLETCHER.'; [94] blank; [95] 'THE
SERAPHIM. | [french rule] | PART THE FIRST.'; [107] 'PART
THE SECOND.'; 133 'EPILOGUE.'; [136] blank; [137] fly title
'PROMETHEUS BOUND.'; [138] blank; [139] text; [191] fly title
'A LAMENT FOR ADONIS. | FROM THE GREEK OF BION.';
[192] blank; [193] text; [199] fly title 'A VISION OF POETS.';
[200] twelve line quotation from 'BRITANNIA'S PASTORALS.';
[201] text; [250] blank; [251] fly title 'THE POET'S VOW. | —O
be wiser thou, | Instructed that true knowledge leads to love. |
WORDSWORTH.'; [252] blank; [253] 'THE POET'S VOW. |
[french rule] | PART THE FIRST.'; 259 'PART THE SECOND.';
265 'PART THE THIRD.'; 267 'PART THE FOURTH.'; 271 'PART
THE FIFTH.'; [277] fly title 'THE ROMAUNT OF MARGRET. |
Can my affections find out nothing best, | But still and still remove?
— | QUARLES.'; [278] blank; [279] text; [290] blank; [291] fly
title 'ISOBEL'S CHILD. | —so find we profit, | By losing of our
prayers. | SHAKESPEARE.'; [292] blank; [293] text; [315] fly title
SONNETS.'; [316] blank; 317 'THE SOUL'S EXPRESSION.'; 318
'THE SERAPH AND POET.'; 319 'BEREAVMENT.'; 320 'CON-
SOLATION.'; 321 'TO MARY RUSSELL MITFORD | IN HER
GARDEN.'; 322 'ON A PORTRAIT OF WORDSWORTH BY | R.
B. HAYDON.'; 323 'PAST AND FUTURE.'; 324 'IRREPARABLE-
NESS.'; 325 'TEARS.'; 326 'GRIEF.'; 327 'SUBSTITUTION.'; 328
'COMFORT.'; 329 'PERPLEXED MUSIC. | AFFECTION-
ATELY INSCRIBED TO. E.J.'; 330 'WORK.'; 331 'FUTURITY.';
332 'THE TWO SAYINGS.'; 333 'THE LOOK.'; 334 'THE MEAN-
ING OF THE LOOK.'; 335 'A THOUGHT FOR A LONELY
DEATH-BED. | INSCRIBED TO MY FRIEND E.C.'; 336
'WORK AND CONTEMPLATION.'; 337 'PAIN IN PLEASURE.';
338 'FLUSH OR FAUNUS.'; 339 'FINITE AND INFINITE.'; 340
'AN APPREHENSION.'; 341 'DISCONTENT.'; 342 'PATIENCE
TAUGHT BY NATURE.'; 343 'CHEERFULNESS TAUGHT BY
REASON.'; 344 'EXAGGERATION.'; 345 'ADEQUACY.'; 346
'TO GEORGE SAND. | A DESIRE.'; 347 'TO GEORGE SAND. |
A RECOGNITION.'; 348 'THE PRISONER.'; 349 'INSUFFI-
CIENCY.'; 350 'TWO SKETCHES. | H.B. | I.'; 351 'A.B. | II.'; 352
'MOUNTAINEER AND POET.'; 353 'THE POET.'; 354 'HIRAM
POWERS' GREEK SLAVE.'; 355 'LIFE.'; 356 'LOVE.'; 357
'HEAVEN AND EARTH.'; 358 'THE PROSPECT.'; 359 'HUGH
STUART BOYD. | HIS BLINDNESS.'; 360 'HUGH STUART
BOYD. | HIS DEATH, 1848.'; 361 'HUGH STUART BOYD. |

LEGACIES.'; [362] 'FUTURE AND PAST.'; [363] printer's imprint.; [364] blank.

Vol. 2. [i] half title 'POEMS.'; [ii] blank; [iii] title page; [iv] printer's imprint; [v] 'CONTENTS.'; [1] 'POEMS. | [*double rule*] | THE ROMAUNT OF THE PAGE.'; [17] 'THE LAY OF THE BROWN ROSARY.'; [39] 'A ROMANCE OF THE GANGES.'; [49] 'RHYME OF THE DUCHESS MAY.'; [80] 'THE ROMANCE OF THE SWAN'S NEST.'; [85] 'BERTHA IN THE LANE.'; [97] 'LADY GERALDINE'S COURTSHIP. | A ROMANCE OF THE AGE.'; [129] 'THE | RUNAWAY SLAVE AT PILGRIM'S POINT.'; [142] 'THE CRY OF THE CHILDREN.'; [150] 'A CHILD ASLEEP.'; [154] 'THE FOURFOLD ASPECT.'; [160] 'NIGHT AND THE MERRY MAN.'; [165] 'EARTH AND HER PRAISERS.'; [174] 'THE VIRGIN MARY TO THE CHILD JESUS.'; [182] 'AN ISLAND.'; [190] 'THE SOUL'S TRAVELLING.'; [199] 'TO BETTINE, | THE CHILD-FRIEND OF GOETHE.'; [202] 'MAN AND NATURE.'; [204] 'A SEA–SIDE WALK.'; [206] 'THE SEA–MEW. | AFFECTIONATELY INSCRIBED TO. M.E.H.'; [209] 'FELICIA HEMANS. | TO L.E.L., REFERRING TO HER MONODY ON THAT POETESS.'; [212] 'L.E.L.'S LAST QUESTION.'; [216] 'CROWNED AND WEDDED.'; [221] 'CROWNED AND BURIED.'; [230] 'TO FLUSH, MY DOG.'; [236] 'THE LOST BOWER.'; [256] 'THE DESERTED GARDEN.'; [261] 'MY DOVES.'; [265] 'HECTOR IN THE GARDEN.'; [270] 'SLEEPING AND WATCHING.'; [273] 'A SONG AGAINST SINGING. | TO E.J.H.'; [276] 'WINE OF CYPRUS.'; [284] 'A RHAPSODY OF LIFE'S PROGRESS.'; [292] 'A LAY OF THE EARLY ROSE.'; [301] 'THE POET AND THE BIRD. | A FABLE.'; [303] 'THE CRY OF THE HUMAN.'; [309] 'A PORTRAIT.'; [312] 'CONFESSIONS.'; [317] 'LOVED ONCE.'; [320] 'THE HOUSE OF CLOUDS.'; [325] 'A SABBATH MORNING AT SEA.'; [329] 'A FLOWER IN A LETTER.'; [335] 'THE MASK.'; [338] 'CALLS ON THE HEART.'; [343] 'WISDOM UNAPPLIED.'; [347] 'MEMORY AND HOPE.'; [350] 'HUMAN LIFE'S MYSTERY.'; [353] 'A CHILD'S THOUGHT OF GOD.'; [355] 'THE CLAIM.'; [357] 'LIFE AND LOVE.'; [358] 'INCLUSIONS.'; [359] 'INSUFFICIENCY.'; [360] 'SONG OF THE ROSE. | ATTRIBUTED TO SAPPHO.'; [361] 'A DEAD ROSE.'; [363] 'THE EXILE'S RETURN.'; [365] 'THE SLEEP.'; [368] 'THE MEASURE.'; [370] 'COWPER'S GRAVE.'; [375] 'SOUNDS.'; [381] 'THE WEAKEST THING.'; [383] 'THE PET-NAME.'; [387] 'THE MOURNING MOTHER | (OF THE DEAD BLIND).'; [391] 'A VALEDICTION.'; [394] LESSONS FROM THE GORSE.'; [396] 'THE LADY'S YES.'; [398] 'A WOMAN'S SHORTCOMINGS.'; [400] 'A MAN'S REQUIREMENTS.'; [403]

'A YEAR'S SPINNING.'; [405] 'CHANGE UPON CHANGE.';
[407] 'THAT DAY.'; [409] 'A REED.'; [410] 'THE DEAD PAN.';
[424] 'A CHILD'S GRAVE AT FLORENCE. | [french rule] |
A.A.E.C. | BORN, JULY, 1848. DIED NOVEMBER, 1849.'; [431]
'CATARINA TO CAMOENS.'; [438] 'SONNETS FROM THE
PORTUGUESE. | I. | I THOUGHT once how Theocritus had
sung'; 439 'II. | BUT only three in all God's universe'; 440 'III. |
UNLIKE are we, unlike, o princely Heart!'; 441 'IV. | THOU hast
thy calling to some palace floor,'; 442 'V. | I LIFT my heavy heart
up solemnly,'; 443 'VI. | GO from me. Yet I feel that I shall stand';
444 'VII. | THE face of all the world is changed, I think,'; 445
'VIII. | WHAT can I give thee back, O liberal'; 446 'IX. | CAN
it be right to give what I can give?'; 447 'X. | YET, love, mere love,
is beautiful indeed'; 448 'XI. | AND therefore if to love can be
desert,'; 449 'XII. | INDEED this very love which is my boast,';
450 'XIII. | AND wilt thou have me fashion into speech'; 451 'XIV.
| IF thou must love me, let it be for nought'; 452 'XV. | ACCUSE
me not, beseech thee, that I wear'; 453 'XVI. | AND yet, because
thou overcomst so,'; 454 'XVII. | MY poet, thou canst touch on all
the notes'; 455 XVIII. | I NEVER gave a lock of hair away'; 456
'XIX. | THE soul's Rialto hath its merchandise;'; 457 'XX. | BE-
LOVED, my Beloved, when I think'; 458 'XXI. | SAY over again
and yet once over again'; 459 'XXII. | WHEN our souls stand up
erect and strong,'; 460 'XXIII. | IS it indeed so? If I lay here dead,';
461 'XXIV. | LET the world's sharpness like a clasping knife'; 462
'XXV. | A HEAVY heart, Beloved, have I borne'; 463 'XXVI. | I
LIVED with visions for my company'; 464 'XXVII. | MY own be-
loved, who hast lifted me'; 465 'XXVIII. | MY letters! all dead pa-
per, . . mute and white!—'; 466 'XXIX. | I THINK of thee!—my
thoughts do twine and bud'; 467 'XXX. | I SEE thine image through
my tears to-night,'; 468 'XXXI. | THOU comest! all is said without a
word'; 469 'XXXII. | THE first time that the sun rose on thine oath';
470 'XXXIII. | YES, call me by my pet-name! let me hear'; 471
'XXXIV. | WITH the same heart, I said, I'll answer thee'; 472
'XXXV. | IF I leave all for thee, wilt thou exchange'; 473 'XXXVI. |
WHEN we first met and loved, I did not build'; 474 'XXXVII. |
PARDON, oh, pardon, that my soul should make'; 475 'XXXVIII.
| FIRST time he kissed me, he but only kissed'; 476 'XXXIX. | BE-
CAUSE thou hast the power and own'st the grace'; 477 'XL. | OH,
yes! they love through all this world of ours!'; 478 'XLI. | I THANK
all who have loved me in their hearts,'; 479 'XLII. | HOW do I love
thee? Let me count the ways.'; 480 'XLIII. | BELOVED, thou has
brought me many flowers'; 'END OF VOL. II.' | [rule] | printer's
imprint.

Typography and paper: Vol. 1 $1,2 signed toward outer margin of foot. Running titles set in rom. caps. with the titles of the individual poems as 'TO FLUSH, MY DOG.' Pagination set in the outer margin of the headline. In the direction line on the first leaf of each gathering is printed 'VOL. I.' Text irregular, 29 lines + headline and direction line. Leaf I2^r measures 12.3 (13.3) × 7.6 cm. Gutter margins measure pp. 120–121 = 2.8 cm; [200]–[201] = 4.0 cm; 264–265 = 4.9 cm. White wove paper unwatermarked. Sheets bulk 2.6 cm. Vol. 2 $1,2 signed with the typographical features of Vol. 1. Gutter margins measure pp. 184–185 = 4.5 cm; 264–265 = 4.9 cm; 344–345 = 4.7 cm. Sheets bulk 3.3 cm.

Binding: Slate green ripple grain (TB) cloth. Sides blind stamped with single rule enclosing an ornate design of leaves. Spine: '[*decorated band*] | ELIZ.^{H} BARRETT | BROWNING'S POEMS | [*short rule*] | VOL. I. [II.] | [*ornate floral design*] | [*thick and thin rule*] | CHAPMAN & HALL | [*thin and thick rule*]' All decoration stamped in blind; all lettering in gilt. Yellow coated end papers. Five stab holes at inner margin. Top and fore edges unopened; bottom edge untrimmed.

Binding variant: As described but there is no publisher's imprint at the foot of the spine. In the same place stamped in gilt 'THIRD EDITION'. (TxU)

Notes: Published October 12, 1853 at sixteen shillings.

Copies examined: MWelC TxU L CLU–C.

A9 : **Two Poems** 1854

[*within a ruled frame*] TWO POEMS. | BY ELIZABETH BARRETT AND ROBERT | BROWNING.

Special imprint: (p. [16] at the center) LONDON: BRADBURY AND EVANS, PRINTERS, WHITEFRIARS.

Collation: 20.2 × 13.5 cm; [A]^8; 8 leaves.

Pagination: [1–3] 4–11 [12–13] 14–15 [16].

Contents: [1] title page; [2] blank; [3] 'A PLEA | FOR | THE RAGGED SCHOOLS OF LONDON.' signed 'ELIZABETH BARRETT BROWNING.' and dated *March 20th*, 1854.'; [12] blank; [13] 'THE TWINS.' signed 'ROBERT BROWNING. | ROME,' and dated *March 30th*, 1854.'; [16] printer's imprint.

Typography and paper: unsigned. Each page enclosed by a ruled frame 14.7 × 8.4 cm. Running titles set in rom. caps. pp. 4–11 above rule, read 'A PLEA FOR THE | RAGGED SCHOOLS OF LONDON.'; pp. 14–15 read 'THE TWINS.' Pagination set in the outer margin of the headline. The single gutter margin measures, pp. 8–9 = 4.7 cm. White wove paper unwatermarked. Sheets bulk 0.1 cm.

Binding: Cream paper wrappers. On front: '[*within a frame of two rules*] TWO POEMS | BY | ELIZABETH BARRETT AND ROBERT | BROWNING. | [*floral ornament*] | LONDON: | CHAPMAN & HALL, 193, PICCADILLY. | 1854.' below the ruled frame is printed '*Price Sixpence*' Back wrapper blank. All edges trimmed.

Notes: Published in April 1854 at sixpence. The cost of printing the pamphlet was paid for by the Brownings and the proceeds were to be given to the Ragged Schools. In all probability the format of this nineteenth century pamphlet suggested that used by Thomas J. Wise for many of his forgeries.

Copies examined: TxU TxWB IU MWelC L O CLU–C.

A10 : Poems Fourth Edition 1856

POEMS. | BY | ELIZABETH BARRETT BROWNING. | FOURTH EDITION. | IN THREE VOLUMES. | VOL. I. [II.] [III.] | LONDON: | CHAPMAN & HALL, 193, PICCADILLY. | 1856.

Special imprints: Vol. 1 (p. [vi] at the center) LONDON: | BRADBURY AND EVANS, PRINTERS, WHITEFRIARS. (p. 314 at the foot) BRADBURY AND EVANS, PRINTERS, WHITEFRIARS. Vol. 2 (p. [iv] and p. [304] at the center) LONDON: | BRADBURY AND EVANS, PRINTERS, WHITE-FRIARS. Vol. 3 (p. [iv] at the center) LONDON: | BRADBURY AND EVANS, PRINTERS WHITEFRIARS. (p. 310 at the foot) BRADBURY AND EVANS, PRINTERS, WHITEFRIARS.

Collation: Vol. 1 17.1 × 10.6 cm; [a]⁴ b² B–U⁸ X⁴ Y²; 164 leaves. Vol. 2 17.1 × 10.6 cm; [A]⁴ B–U⁸; 156 leaves. Vol. 3 17.1 × 10.6 cm; [A]⁴ B–U⁸ X⁴; 160 leaves.

Pagination: Vol. 1 [i–vii] viii [ix–xii], [1–3] 4–92 [93–95] 96–106 [107] 108–135 [136–139] 140–190 [191–193] 194–198 [199–201] 202–249 [250–253] 254–276 [277–279] 280–289 [290–293] 294–314 [2]. Vol. 2 [i–v] vi–viii, [1] 2–16 [17] 18–38 [39] 40–48 [49] 50–79 [80] 81–84 [85] 86–96 [97] 98–128 [129] 130–141 [142] 143–149 [150] 151–153 [154] 155–159 [160] 161–164 [165] 166–173 [174] 175–181 [182] 183–189 [190] 191–198 [199] 200–201 [202]

203 [204] 205 [206] 207–208 [209] 210–211 [212] 213–215 [216]
217–220 [221] 222–229 [230] 231–235 [236] 237–240 [241] 242–244
[245] 246–249 [250] 251–252 [253] 254–303 [304]. Vol. 3 [i–v] vi–
vii [viii], [1] 2–20 [21] 22–23 [24] 25–31 [32] 33–39 [40] 41–48
[49] 50 [51] 52–56 [57] 58–59 [60] 61–65 [66] 67–68 [69] 70–73
[74] 75–77 [78] 79–83 [84] 85–86 [87] 88–91 [92] 93–95 [96] 97–
98 [99] 100–101 [102] 103 [104] 105 [106–107] 108 [109] 110
[111] 112–113 [114] 115 [116] 117–120 [121] 122 [123] 124–126
[127] 128–130 [131] 132–133 [134] 135 [136] 137 [138] 139 [140]
141–142 [143] 144 [145] 146 [147] 148 [149–150] 151–163 [164]
165–170 [171] 172–177 [178–179] 180–181 [182] 183–184 [185–
188] 189–231 [232–235] 236 [237] 238–310 [311–312].

Contents: Vol. 1 1 blank leaf; [iii] half title 'POEMS.'; [iv] blank;
[v] title page; [vi] printer's imprint; [vii] '𝔇𝔢𝔡𝔦𝔠𝔞𝔱𝔦𝔬𝔫.' | [*french
rule*] | TO MY FATHER.'; [ix] 'ADVERTISEMENT.' signed
'LONDON, 1856.'; [x] blank; [xi] 'CONTENTS.'; [xii] blank; [1]
fly title 'A DRAMA OF EXILE.'; [2] blank; [3] text; [93] fly title
'THE SERAPHIM.' | I Look for Angels' songs, and hear Him cry.
| GILES FLETCHER.'; [94] blank; [95] 'THE SERAPHIM. |
[*french rule*] | PART THE FIRST.'; [107] 'PART THE SEC-
OND.'; 133 'EPILOGUE.'; [136] blank; [137] fly title 'PRO-
METHEUS BOUND. | FROM THE GREEK OF ÆSCHYLUS.';
[138] blank; [139] text; [191] fly title 'A LAMENT FOR ADONIS.
| FROM THE GREEK OF BION.'; [192] blank; [193] text; [199]
fly title 'A VISION OF POETS.'; [200] twelve line quotation from
'BRITANNIA'S PASTORALS.'; [201] text; [250] blank; [251] fly
title 'THE POET'S VOW. | —O be wiser thou, | Instructed that
true knowledge leads to love. | WORDSWORTH.'; [252] blank;
[253] 'THE POET'S VOW. | [*french rule*] | PART THE FIRST.';
259 'PART THE SECOND.'; 265 'PART THE THIRD.'; 267
'PART THE FOURTH.'; 271 'PART THE FIFTH.' [277] fly title
'THE ROMAUNT OF MARGRET. | Can my affections find out
nothing best, | But still and still remove? — | QUARLES.'; [278]
blank; [279] text; [290] blank; [291] fly title 'ISOBEL'S CHILD.'
| —so find we profit, | By losing of our prayers. | SHAKE-
SPEARE.'; [292] blank; [293] text; 314 'END OF VOL. I.', printer's imprint; 1 blank leaf.

Vol. 2 [i] half title 'POEMS.'; [ii] blank; [iii] title page; [iv]
printer's imprint; [v] 'CONTENTS.'; [1] 'POEMS. | [*double rule*]
| THE ROMAUNT OF THE PAGE.'; [17] 'THE LAY OF THE
BROWN ROSARY.'; [39] 'A ROMANCE OF THE GANGES.';
[49] 'RHYME OF THE DUCHESS MAY.'; [80] 'THE RO-
MANCE OF THE SWAN'S NEST.'; [85] 'BERTHA IN THE
LANE.'; [97] 'LADY GERALDINE'S COURTSHIP. | A RO-

MANCE OF THE AGE.'; [129] 'THE | RUNAWAY SLAVE AT
PILGRIM'S POINT.'; [142] 'THE CRY OF THE CHILDREN.';
[150] 'A CHILD ASLEEP.'; [154] 'THE FOURFOLD ASPECT.';
[160] 'NIGHT AND THE MERRY MAN.'; [165] 'EARTH AND
HER PRAISERS.'; [174] 'THE VIRGIN MARY TO THE CHILD
JESUS.'; [182] 'AN ISLAND.'; [190] 'THE SOUL'S TRAVEL-
LING.'; [199] 'TO BETTINE, | THE CHILD-FRIEND OF
GOETHE.'; [202] 'MAN AND NATURE.'; [204] 'A SEA-SIDE
WALK.'; [206] 'THE SEA-MEW. | AFFECTIONATELY IN-
SCRIBED TO M.E.H.'; [209] 'FELICIA HEMANS. | TO L.E.L.,
REFERRING TO HER MONODY ON THE POETESS.'; [212]
'L.E.L.'S LAST QUESTION.'; [216] 'CROWNED AND
WEDDED.'; [221] 'CROWNED AND BURIED.'; [230] 'TO
FLUSH, MY DOG.'; [236] 'THE DESERTED GARDEN.'; [241]
'MY DOVES.'; [245] 'HECTOR IN THE GARDEN.'; [250]
'SLEEPING AND WATCHING.'; [253] 'SOUNDS.'; 259 'THE
SOUL'S EXPRESSION.'; 260 'THE SERAPH AND THE POET.';
261 'BEREAVEMENT.'; 262 'CONSOLATION.'; 263 'TO MARY
RUSSELL MITFORD | IN HER GARDEN.'; 264 'ON A POR-
TRAIT OF WORDSWORTH BY | R. B. HAYDON.'; 265 'PAST
AND FUTURE.'; 266 'IRREPARABLENESS.'; 267 'TEARS.'; 268
'GRIEF.'; 269 'SUBSTITUTION.'; 270 'COMFORT.'; 271 'PER-
PLEXED MUSIC. | AFFECTIONATELY INSCRIBED TO E.J.';
272 'WORK.'; 273 'FUTURITY.'; 274 'THE TWO SAYINGS.'; 275
'THE LOOK.'; 276 'THE MEANING OF THE LOOK.'; 277 'A
THOUGHT FOR A LONELY DEATH-BED. | INSCRIBED TO
MY FRIEND E. C.'; 278 'WORK AND CONTEMPLATION.';
279 'PAIN IN PLEASURE.'; 280 'FLUSH OR FAUNUS.'; 281
'FINITE AND INFINITE.'; 282 'AN APPREHENSION.'; 283
'DISCONTENT.'; 284 'PATIENCE TAUGHT BY NATURE.';
285 'CHEERFULNESS TAUGHT BY REASON.'; 286 'EXAG-
GERATION.'; 287 'ADEQUACY.'; 288 'TO GEORGE SAND. | A
DESIRE.'; 289 'TO GEORGE SAND. | A RECOGNITION.'; 290
'THE PRISONER.'; 291 'INSUFFICIENCY.'; 292 ' TWO
SKETCHES. | H.B. | I.'; 293 'A.B. | II.'; 294 'MOUNTAINEER
AND POET.'; 295 'THE POET.'; 296 'HIRAM POWERS'
GREEK SLAVE.'; 297 'LIFE.'; 298 'LOVE.'; 299 'HEAVEN AND
EARTH.'; 300 'THE PROSPECT.'; 301 'HUGH STUART BOYD.
| HIS BLINDNESS.'; 302 'HUGH STUART BOYD. | HIS
DEATH, 1848.'; 303 'HUGH STUART BOYD. | LEGACIES.';
'END OF VOL. II.'; 304 printer's imprint.

Vol. 3 [i] half title 'POEMS.'; [ii] blank; [iii] title page; [iv] print-
er's imprint; [v] 'CONTENTS.'; [viii] blank; [1] 'POEMS. |
[double rule] | THE LOST BOWER.'; [21] 'A SONG AGAINST

SINGING. | TO E.J.H.'; [24] 'WINE OF CYPRUS.'; [32] 'A RHAPSODY OF LIFE'S PROGRESS.'; [40] 'A LAY OF THE EARLY ROSE.'; [49] 'THE POET AND THE BIRD. | A FABLE.'; [51] 'THE CRY OF THE HUMAN.'; [57] 'A PORTRAIT.'; [60] 'CONFESSIONS.'; [66] 'LOVED ONCE.'; [69] 'THE HOUSE OF CLOUDS.'; [74] 'A SABBATH MORNING AT SEA.'; [78] 'A FLOWER IN A LETTER.'; [84] 'THE MASK.'; [87] 'CALLS ON THE HEART.'; [92] 'WISDOM UNAPPLIED.'; [96] 'MEM-ORY AND HOPE.'; [99] 'HUMAN LIFE'S MYSTERY.'; [102] 'A CHILD'S THOUGHT OF GOD.'; [104] 'THE CLAIM.'; [106] 'SONG OF THE ROSE. | ATTRIBUTED TO SAPPHO.'; [107] 'A DEAD ROSE.'; [109] 'THE EXILE'S RETURN.'; [111] 'THE SLEEP.'; [114] 'THE MEASURE.'; [116] COWPER'S GRAVE.'; [121] 'THE WEAKEST THING.'; [123] 'THE PET NAME.'; [127] 'THE MOURNING MOTHER | (OF THE DEAD BLIND).'; [131] 'A VALEDICTION.'; [134] 'LESSONS FROM THE GORSE.'; [136] 'THE LADY'S YES.'; [138] 'A WOMAN'S SHORTCOMINGS.'; [140] 'A MAN'S REQUIREMENTS.'; [143] 'A YEAR'S SPINNING.'; [145] 'CHANGE UPON CHANGE.'; [147] 'THAT DAY.'; [149] 'A REED.'; [150] 'THE DEAD PAN.'; [164] 'A CHILD'S GRAVE AT FLORENCE | [*french rule*] | A.A.E.C. | BORN, JULY, 1848. DIED NOVEMBER, 1849.'; [171] 'CATARINA TO CAMOENS.'; [178] 'LIFE AND LOVE.'; [179] 'A DENIAL.'; [182] 'PROOF AND DISPROOF.'; [185] 'QUES-TION AND ANSWER.'; [186] 'INCLUSIONS.'; [187] 'INSUF-FICIENCY.'; 188 'SONNETS FROM THE PORTUGUESE. | [*french rule*] | I. | I THOUGHT once how Theocritus had sung'; 189 'II. | BUT only three in all God's universe'; 190 'III. | UNLIKE are we, unlike, O princely Heart!'; 191 'IV. | THOU hast thy call-ing to some palace floor,'; 192 'V. | I LIFT my heavy heart up solemnly,'; 193 'VI. | GO from me. Yet I feel that I shall stand'; 194 'VII. | THE face of all the world is changed, I think,'; 195 'VIII. | WHAT can I give thee back, O liberal'; 196 'IX. | CAN it be right to give what I can give?'; 197 'X. | YET, love, mere love, is beauti-ful indeed'; 198 'XI. | AND therefore if to love can be desert,'; 199 'XII. | INDEED this very love which is my boast,'; 200 'XIII. | AND wilt thou have me fashion into speech'; 201 'XIV. | IF thou must love me, let it be for nought'; 202 'XV. | ACCUSE me not, beseech thee, that I wear'; 203 'XVI. | AND yet, because thou overcomest so,'; 204 'XVII. | MY poet, thou canst touch on all the notes'; 205 'XVIII. | I NEVER gave a lock of hair away'; 206 'XIX. | THE soul's Rialto hath its merchandise;'; 207 'XX. | BELOVED, my Beloved, when I think'; 208 'XXI. | SAY over again, and yet once over again,'; 209 'XXII. | WHEN our two souls stand up erect and strong,'; 210 'XXIII. | IS it indeed so? If I lay here dead,';

211 'XXIV. | LET the world's sharpness like a clasping knife'; 212
'XXV. | A HEAVY heart, Belovèd, have I borne'; 213 'XXVI. | I
LIVED with visions for my company,'; 214 'XXVII. | MY own be-
lovèd, who has lifted me'; 215 'XXVIII. | MY letters! all dead
papers, . . mute and white!—'; 216 'XXIX. | I THINK of thee!—my
thoughts do twine and bud'; 217 'XXX. | I SEE thine image through
my tears to-night,'; 218 'XXXI. | THOU comest! all is said without
a word.'; 219 'XXXII. | THE first time that the sun rose on thine
oath'; 220 'XXXIII. | YES, call me by my pet-name! let me hear';
221 'XXXIV. | WITH the same heart, I said, I'll answer thee'; 222
'XXXV. | IF I leave all for thee, wilt thou exchange'; 223 'XXXVI. |
WHEN we met first and loved, I did not build'; 224 'XXXVII. |
PARDON, oh pardon, that my soul should make'; 225 'XXXVIII. |
FIRST time he kissed me, he but only kissed'; 226 'XXXIX. | BE-
CAUSE thou hast the power and own'st the grace'; 227 'XL. | OH,
Yes! they love through all this world of ours!'; 228 'XLI. | I THANK
all who have loved me in their hearts,'; 229 'XLII. | 'My future will
not copy fair my past'—'; 230 'XLIII. | HOW do I love thee? Let
me count the ways,'; 231 |XLIV. | BELOVÈD, thou hast brought
me many flowers'; [232] blank; [233] fly title 'CASA GUIDI
WINDOWS. | A Poem, | IN TWO PARTS.'; [234] blank; [235]
'ADVERTISEMENT TO THE FIRST EDITION.'; [237] 'CASA
GUIDI WINDOWS. | [french rule] | 'PART I.'; 282 'PART II.';
310 'THE END.', printer's imprint; [311] advertisement for five
titles from 'AURORA LEIGH.' to 'CHRISTMAS-EVE AND
EASTER-DAY.'; [312] blank.

Typography and paper: Vol. 1 $1,2 signed toward outer margin
of foot. Running titles set in rom. caps. with the titles of the individual poems as 'LADY GERALDINE'S COURTSHIP.' Pagination set in the outer margin of the headline. In the direction line
on the first leaf of each gathering is printed 'VOL. I.' Text irregular,
29 lines + headline and direction line. Leaf N1^r type page measures 12.4 (13.4) × 7.6 cm. Gutter margins measure, pp. 120–121 =
2.5 cm; 168–169 = 2.4 cm; 216–217 = 4.4 cm. White wove paper
unwatermarked. Sheets bulk 2.3 cm. Vol. 2 $1,2 signed with the
typographical features of Vol. 1. Gutter margins measure pp. 152–
153 = 2.7 cm; 184–185 = 4.7 cm; [216]–217 = 2.7 cm. Sheets bulk
2.3 cm. Vol. 3 $1,2 signed with the typographical features of Vols.
1 & 2. Gutter margins measure pp. 152–153 = 5.0 cm; 216–217 =
3.2 cm; 308–309 = 2.8 cm. Sheets bulk 2.3 cm.

Binding: Green morocco like (AR) cloth. Sides blind stamped
with a frame of two rules enclosing an ornately decorated rec-
tangle. Spine :"[*conventional decorated band*] | ELIZ^H BARRETT
| BROWNING'S | POEMS | [*short rule*] | VOL. I. [II.] [III.] |

[*ornament*] | CHAPMAN & HALL | [*conventional decorated band*]' All in gilt. Five stab holes at inner margin. Top and fore edges unopened; bottom edge untrimmed.

Notes: Published November 1, 1856 at eighteen shillings. In addition to revising the text of twenty poems, adding three new poems and three translations, the whole of "Casa Guidi Windows" was revised. Also the order of the "Sonnets from the Portuguese" was changed. The sonnet, "FUTURE AND PAST." which was printed in the earlier editions of E.B.B.'s poems became sonnet XLII in the sequence. Sonnets XLII and XLIII became sonnets XLIII and XLIV respectively.

Copies examined: TxU MWelC L CLU–C.

A11 : Aurora Leigh 1857

AURORA LEIGH. | BY | ELIZABETH BARRETT BROWNING. | LONDON: | CHAPMAN AND HALL, 193, PICCADILLY. | 1857.

Special imprints: (p. [vi] at the center) LONDON: | BRADBURY AND EVANS, PRINTERS, WHITEFRIARS. (p. 403 at the foot) BRADBURY AND EVANS, PRINTERS, WHITEFRIARS.

Collation: 19.0 × 12.4 cm; [A]⁴ B–CC⁸ DD²; 206 leaves.

Pagination: [i–viii], [1] 2–41 [42–43] 44–88 [89] 90–133 [134–135] 136–179 [180–181] 182–227 [228–229] 230–274 [275] 276–321 [322–323] 324–368 [369] 370–403 [404].

Contents: [i] blank; [ii] advertisement for four titles from '*The Fourth Edition of* | ELIZABETH BARRETT BROWNING'S POEMS.' to 'CHRISTMAS-EVE AND EASTER-DAY.'; [iii] half title 'AURORA LEIGH.'; [iv] blank; [v] title page; [vi] printer's imprint; [vii] 𝕯𝖊𝖉𝖎𝖈𝖆𝖙𝖎𝖔𝖓 | TO | JOHN KENYON, ESQ.' signed 'E.B.B. | 39 DEVONSHIRE PLACE,' and dated '*October* 17, 1856.'; [viii] blank; [1] 'AURORA LEIGH. | [*double rule*] | FIRST BOOK.'; [42] blank; [43] 'SECOND BOOK.'; [89] 'THIRD BOOK.'; [134] blank; [135] 'FOURTH BOOK.'; [180] blank; [181] 'FIFTH BOOK.'; [228] blank; [229] 'SIXTH BOOK.'; [275] 'SEVENTH BOOK.'; [322] blank; [323] 'EIGHTH BOOK.'; [369] 'NINTH BOOK.'; 403 'THE END.', printer's imprint; [404] blank.

Typography and paper: $1,2 signed toward outer margin of foot. Running titles set in rom. caps. as 'AURORA LEIGH.' Pagination set in the outer margin of the headline. Text 30 lines + headline and direction line. Leaf Ml^r type page measures 14.1 (15.1) × 8.4 cm. Gutter margins measure pp. 168–169 = 4.0 cm; 200–201 = 4.7 cm; 232–233 = 4.6 cm. White wove paper unwatermarked. Sheets bulk 2.7 cm.

Binding: Red morocco like (AR) cloth. Also green morocco like (AR) cloth. Sides blind stamped with a border of three rules enclosing a boxed floral design. Spine: '[*conventional decorated band*] | AURORA LEIGH | [*rule*] | ELIZABETH | BARRETT BROWNING | [*two floral devices*] | CHAPMAN & HALL | [*conventional decorated band*]'. All in gilt. Yellow coated end papers. Five stab holes at inner margin. Top and fore edges unopened; bottom edge untrimmed. In some copies leaf A1 on which the advertisements are printed has been excised and tipped in following leaf DD2.

Notes: Published November 15, 1856 at twelve shillings. The title page is dated 1857, but the practice of post dating editions was commonplace in the trade at this time. Contemporary advertisements note the book's publication in 1856 and presentation copies at Iowa and the Berg Collection are inscribed 1856. An incomplete set of page proofs with corrections are at the Bodleian library. Manuscripts are at Harvard and Wellesley.

First impression

As described with the following points: Line 29 page 106 reads ". . . there 's the worst". Line 12 page 133 reads ". . . he 'd remember her's," Line 7 page 144 reads "You 're slow . . ."; line 8 page 144 reads "I 've waited . . ."; line 17 page 144 reads ". . . we 've grown,". The distance from Sig CC2 to the headline is 15.1 cm. (CLU–C)

Second impression

As described with these variants: Line 29 page 106 corrected to read ". . . there's the worst." Line 12 page 133 corrected to read ". . . he'd remember hers,". Line 7 page 144 corrected to read "You're slow . . ."; line 8 page 144 corrected to read "I've waited . . ."; line 17 page 144 corrected to read ". . . we've grown,". The distance from Sig CC2 to the headline is 15.1 cm.

Third Impression

Pages 106, 133, and 144 corrected as in the second impression, but every page of gathering CC has been reset. The distance from Sig CC2 to the headline is 15.2 cm. (NIC)
Copies with mixed sheets have been seen in the following combina-

tions: Page 106 uncorrected; page 133, 144 corrected. (TxWB) Page 106 corrected; pages 133, 144 uncorrected. (TxU). Pages 106, 133 corrected; page 144 uncorrected (CSMH)

Copies examined: NIC NN MH MB MWelC DLC IU IaU ICU ICN TxU TxWB L O CLU–C CSmH.

A11a : Aurora Leigh 1857

First American edition

AURORA LEIGH. | BY | ELIZABETH BARRETT BROWNING. | [*ornamental rule* 2.9 *cm.*] | NEW YORK: | C. S. FRANCIS & CO., 554 BROADWAY. | BOSTON:—53 DEVONSHIRE STREET. | 1857.

Special imprints: none.

Collation: 18.0 × 11.5 cm; π^4 A–U^8 [ ]^8 X–Y^8; $\langle\pi^4$ 1–30^6 31$^4\rangle$; 188 leaves.

Pagination: [i–viii], [1] 2–38 [39] 40–80 [81] 82–121 [122] 123–163 [164]165–206 [207] 208–248 [249] 250–291 [292] 293–334 [335] 336–366 [2].

Contents: [i] half title 'AURORA LEIGH.'; [ii] blank; [iii] title page; [iv] blank; [v] 'AUTHOR'S EDITION. | [*rule*] | Having received what I consider to be sufficient remuneration for | my poem of "AURORA LEIGH," from Mr. FRANCIS, of New York, it | is my earnest desire that his right in this and future editions of the | same, may not be interfered with. | ELIZABETH BARRETT BROWNING. | LONDON, *Oct.* 21, 1856.'; [vi] blank; [vii] 'Dedication | TO | JOHN KENYON, ESQ.' signed 'E.B.B. | 39 DEVONSHIRE PLACE,' and dated '*October* 17, 1856.'; [viii] blank; [1] 'AURORA LEIGH. | [*rule*] | FIRST BOOK.'; [39] 'SECOND BOOK.'; [81] 'THIRD BOOK.'; [122] 'FOURTH BOOK.'; [164] 'FIFTH BOOK.'; [207] 'SIXTH BOOK.'; [249] 'SEVENTH BOOK.'; [292] 'EIGHTH BOOK.'; [335] 'NINTH BOOK.'; 366 'THE END.' 1 blank leaf.

Typography and paper: alphabetical signatures $1 signed toward outer margin of foot; numerical signatures (–29$_1$, 31$_1$) $1,3* signed toward inner margin of foot. Leaf 08 missigned I. Leaf 12$_3$ missigned 12*. Running titles set in rom. caps. as 'AURORA LEIGH.' Pagination set in the outer margin of the headline. Text irregular, 33 lines + headline and direction line. Leaf QI^r type page measures 13.3 (14.3) × 7.1+ cm. Gutter margins measure pp. 168–169 = 4.5 cm; 200–201 = 4.5 cm; 232–233 = 4.5 cm. White wove paper unwatermarked. Sheets bulk 2.9 cm.

Binding: Brown vertically ribbed (T) cloth. Sides blind stamped with a frame of three rules with corner points enclosing a centered arabesque. Spine: '[rule] | [double rule] | AURORA LEIGH | [short rule] | MRS. BROWNING | [double rule] | [double rule] | [double rule] | [rule] | FRANCIS & CO. | [double rule].' All lettering and short rule stamped in gilt; other rules stamped in blind. Pale yellow end papers. Single binder's leaf at front and back. Four stab holes at inner margin. All edges trimmed.

Notes: Advertised *New York Tribune*, 10 November 1856, "In Press: Mrs. Browning's New Poem, Aurora Leigh, from advance sheets, simultaneously with the London edition." The price was $1.00. Certain changes made by E.B.B. to the page proofs of the English edition appear in the American edition: page 18, line 27 ". . . and leave the world a stink" to ". . . and leave the world a dusk"; page 275, line 10 "A motherly right damnable good turn" to "A motherly, unmercifully, good turn". This would indicate the American edition for which Francis paid E.B.B. £100 was published from corrected proof sheets, rather than a fair copy of the manuscript.

First Impression

As described. but with these variants. Collation: π^4 ($-\pi^4$) A–U⁸ [ ]⁸ X–Y⁸; ⟨π^4 ($-\pi^4$) 1–30⁶ 31⁴⟩ . Leafπ^4 excised. The contents of this gathering arranged as follows: [i] half title; [ii] blank; [iii] title page; [iv] Author's Edition; [v] Dedication; [vi] blank. The height of the leaves is 18.5 cm. (DLC)

Second Impression

As described. (TxU)

Third Impression

As described. Collation as in second impression, but page [ii] contains advertisements for three titles from 'POEMS' to 'Aurora Leigh'. The height of the leaves is 18.1 cm. (CSMH)

Copies examined: NN MWelC DLC TxU TxWB WB CLU–C CSMH

A11b : Aurora Leigh 1859

Revised Edition

AURORA LEIGH. | BY | ELIZABETH BARRETT BROWNING.

| FOURTH EDITION. | *REVISED.* | LONDON: | CHAPMAN AND HALL, 193 PICCADILLY. | 1859.

Special imprints: (p. [ii] at the foot) LONDON: PRINTED BY WILLIAM CLOWES AND SONS, STAMFORD STREET. (p. 403 at the foot) imprint as above.

Collation: 17.0 × 10.7 cm; [A]² B–2C⁸ 2D²; 204 leaves + 1 plate.

Pagination: [i–iv], [1] 2–41 [42] 43–133 [134] 135–179 [180] 181–227 [228] 229–321 [322] 323–403 [404].

Contents: [i] title page; [ii] printer's imprint; [iii] 'Dedication | TO | JOHN KENYON, ESQ.' signed 'E.B.B. | 39, DEVONSHIRE PLACE,' and dated '*October* 17, 1856.'; [iv] blank; [1] 'AURORA LEIGH. | [*double rule*] | FIRST BOOK.'; [42] blank; 43 'SECOND BOOK.'; 89 'THIRD BOOK.'; [134] blank; 135 'FOURTH BOOK.'; [180] blank; 181 'FIFTH BOOK.'; [228] blank; 229 'SIXTH BOOK.'; 275 'SEVENTH BOOK.'; [322] blank; 323 'EIGHTH BOOK.'; 369 'NINTH BOOK.'; 403 'THE END.', printer's imprint; [404] blank.

Typography and paper: $1 signed toward outer margin of foot. Running titles set in rom. caps. as 'AURORA LEIGH.' Pagination set in the outer margin of the headline except pages 43, 89, 135, 181, 229, 275, 323, 369 which are enclosed in parentheses and centered at the top. Text irregular, 30 lines + headline and direction line. Leaf Xl^r type page measures 12.1+ (13.2) × 8.0 cm. Gutter margins measure, pp. 120–121 = 2.5 cm; 280–281 = 2.8 cm; 328–329 = 2.6 cm. White wove paper unwatermarked. Sheets bulk 2.5 cm.

Plate: Pasted to leaf [Al^r] is an engraved portrait frontispiece of E.B.B.

Binding: Green morocco like (AR) cloth. Sides blind stamped with a frame of three rules enclosing a rectangular arabesque. Spine: '[*conventional decorated band*] | AURORA | LEIGH. | [*short rule*] | ELIZ^H BARRETT | BROWNING. | [*ornament*] | CHAPMAN & HALL | [*conventional decorated band*]'. All in gilt. Yellow coated end papers. Four stab holes at inner margin. On pastedown at back, binder's stamp reads 'BOUND BY BONE & SON, 76 FLEET STREET LONDON.' Top and fore edges unopened; bottom edge untrimmed.

Notes: Published June 11, 1859 at twelve shillings. At her publisher's request E.B.B. made a number of revisions for this edition. Collation indicates they were of a minor stylistic nature. The acci-

dentals are changed considerably following the house style of
William Clowes, rather than Bradbury and Evans, printers of the
previous editions. Corrected proof sheets at Lilly Library. Presentation copy with ms. corrections in the hand of the author at Yale.

Copies examined: IU L.

A12 : Poems Before Congress 1860

POEMS BEFORE CONGRESS. | BY | ELIZABETH BARRETT
BROWNING. | LONDON: | CHAPMAN AND HALL, 193 PIC-
CADILLY. | 1860.

Special imprint: (p. [iv] at the center) LONDON: | BRADBURY
AND EVANS, PRINTERS, WHITEFRIARS.

Collation: 19.0 × 12.4 cm; [A]⁶ B–E⁸ F²; 40 leaves.

Pagination: [2] [i–v] vi–viii [ix–x], [1] 2–65 [66–68].

Contents: 1 blank leaf; [i] half title 'POEMS BEFORE CON-
GRESS.'; [ii] blank; [iii] title page; [iv] printer's imprint; [v]
'PREFACE.' signed 'Rome, *February*, 1860.'; [ix] 'CONTENTS.';
[x] blank; [1] 'POEMS BEFORE CONGRESS. | [*double rule*] |
NAPOLEON III IN ITALY.'; 21 'THE DANCE.'; 26 'A TALE OF
VILLAFRANCA.'; 32 'A COURT LADY.'; 39 'AN AUGUST
VOICE.'; 46 'CHRISTMAS GIFTS.'; 50 'ITALY AND THE
WORLD.'; 59 'A CURSE FOR A NATION.'; [66] blank; [67]
advertisement for five titles headed 'MRS. BROWNING.' to 'MEN
AND WOMEN. | BY ROBERT BROWNING.'; [68] blank.

Typography and paper: $1,2 signed toward outer margin of foot.
Running titles set in rom. caps. with the titles of the individual
poems as 'ITALY AND THE WORLD.' Pagination set in the outer
margin of the headline except pages 26, 32, 39, 46, 50, 59 which are
centered. Text irregular, 23 lines + headline and direction line.
Leaf B2ʳ type page measures 13.8 (15.1) × 7.3 cm. Gutter margins
measure pp. 24–25 = 3.9 cm; 40–41 = 5.9 cm; 56–57 = 4.3 cm. On
page 37 the second roman numeral X in stanzas XX and XXIII is
from a smaller font of type than that used elsewhere.

Binding: Red morocco-like (AR) cloth. Sides blind stamped with
a frame of four rules enclosing an arabesque design. On the front:
'POEMS BEFORE CONGRESS | [*rule*] | ELIZABETH BAR-
RETT BROWNING'. All in gilt. No stamping on the back or
spine. Brown coated end papers. In some copies a publisher's catalogue of 32 pages dated February 1860 is present. Four stab holes

at inner margin. Top and fore edges unopened; bottom edge untrimmed.

Notes: Published March 12, 1860 at four shillings. The manuscript is at the University of Texas. A copy of the published book containing ms corrections in the hand of the author is at Yale.

Two impressions

A. As described with the following points: Line 1 page 25 reads '. . . different: scarce'. (TxU)

B. As described with this variant: Lines 1, 2, 3, 5 on page 25 show resetting and line 1 reads: ". . . different : scarce". (TxWB)
The width of several type pages in the two impressions is as follows:

Page line	A	B
5.19	7.3	7.2+
23.10	8.0+	8.0
60.20	6.3+	6.2+

Copies examined: MH MB MWelC NN DLC IU ICU TxU TxWB L O CLU–C.

A12a : Napoleon III in Italy 1860

NAPOLEON III | IN ITALY. | AND OTHER POEMS. | BY | ELIZABETH BARRETT BROWNING. | [*ornamental rule 2.0 cm.*] | NEW YORK: | C. S. FRANCIS & CO., 544 BROADWAY. | 1860.

Special imprint: (p. [2] at the foot) PRINTED BY | C. S. FRANCIS & CO., BOSTON.

Collation: 17.5 × 11.4 cm; [1]⁶ 2–3⁶ [4–6]⁶; 36 leaves.

Pagination: [1–3] 4–6 [7–9] 10–28 [29] 30–33 [34] 35–38 [39] 40–45 [46] 47–52 [53] 54–56 [57] 58–65 [66] 67–72.

Contents: [1] title page; [2] [*rule*] | 'AUTHORS EDITION.' | [*rule*] | 'This volume is published in England under the title of | "Poems before Congress." ' | [*rule*] | printer's imprint.; [3] 'PREFACE.' dated 'ROME, *February*, 1860.'; [7] 'CONTENTS.'; [8] blank; [9] 'POEMS. | [*rule*] | NAPOLEON III. IN ITALY.'; [29] 'THE DANCE.'; [34] 'A TALE OF VILLAFRANCA. | TOLD IN TUSCANY.'; [39] 'A COURT LADY.'; [46] 'AN AUGUST VOICE.'; [53] 'CHRISTMAS GIFTS.'; [57] 'ITALY AND THE WORLD.'; [66] 'A CURSE FOR A NATION.'

Typography and paper: $1,3* signed toward inner margin of foot. Leaf 2₃ also signed B. Running titles set in rom. caps. with the titles of the individual poems as 'NAPOLEON III. IN ITALY.' Pagination set in the outer margin of the headline. Text irregular, 25 lines + headline and direction line. Leaf 3₁ʳ type page measures 13.3 (14.1) × 7.1 cm. On page 59 stanza IX. is misnumbered XI. Gutter margins measure pp. 6–[7] = 3.5 cm; 30–31 = 3.6 cm; 42–43 = 3.6 cm. White wove paper unwatermarked. Sheets bulk 0.6+ cm.

Binding: Brown ripple grain (TZ) cloth. Sides blind stamped with a frame of four rules having decorative centerpieces and corner points. Front: 'Napoleon III. | IN ITALY | etc. | [*rule*] | Mrs. BROWNING'. All in gilt. Thick and thin rules at head and foot of spine in gilt. No lettering. Yellow end papers. Single binder's leaf at front and back. Four stab holes at inner margin. At back a publisher's catalogue of 8 pages advertising New and Standard Books published by C. S. Francis is inserted. All edges trimmed. Also in brown, red, blue vertically ribbed (T) cloth with the same stamping. (TxWB).

Notes: Advertised *New York Tribune* 30 March 1860 "Ready next week." Advertised *Tribune* 4 April 1860 at $.50. C. S. Francis wished to publish the edition as *Napoleon III in Italy* rather than with the title of the English edition, *Poems Before Congress*. Collation between the two editions indicates the American edition set from sheets of the English edition.

Two Impressions

A. As described with the following points: In Sig 2 the height of the type page 13 (less headline) = 12.9 cm.; 14 = 12.7+ cm; 15 = 11.1 cm; 16 = 12.8 cm; 18 = 12.9 cm; 21 = 12.7 cm; 22 = 12.8 cm; 23 = 12.2+ cm. Also page 39 = 8.6+ cm; 44 = 12.0 cm; 60 = 13.0 cm. (WB)

B. As described with these variants: In Sig 2 the height of the type page 13 = 13.0 cm; 14 = 12.8 cm; 15 = 11.2 cm; 16 = 12.9 cm; 18 = 13.0 cm; 21 = 12.8+ cm; 22 = 12.9 cm; 23 = 12.3 cm; Also page 39 = 8.7+ cm; 44 = 12.1 cm; 60 = 13.1 cm. (TxU)

Copies examined: TxU TxWB WB.

A13 : Last Poems 1862

LAST POEMS | BY | ELIZABETH BARRETT BROWNING. | LONDON: | CHAPMAN AND HALL, 193, PICCADILLY. | 1862.

Special imprints: (p. [iv] at the center) PRINTED BY | JOHN EDWARD TAYLOR, LITTLE QUEEN STREET, | LINCOLN'S INN FIELDS. (p. 142 at the foot) JOHN EDWARD TAYLOR, PRINTER, | LITTLE QUEEN STREET, LINCOLN'S INN FIELDS.

Collation: 19.0 × 12.5 cm; [a]⁴ b² B–K⁸; 78 leaves.

Pagination: [i–ix] x–xi [xii], [1] 2–102 [103–104] 105–142 [143–144].

Contents: [i] half title 'LAST POEMS.'; [ii] blank; [iii] title page; [iv] printer's imprint; [v] dedication 'TO "GRATEFUL FLOR-ENCE," | TO THE MUNICIPALITY, HER REPRESENTATIVE, | AND TO TOMMASEO, ITS SPOKESMAN, | MOST GRATE-FULLY.'; [vi] blank; [vii] 'ADVERTISEMENT' dated 'LON-DON, *February*, 1862.'; [viii] blank; [ix] 'CONTENTS.'; [xii] blank; [1] 'LAST POEMS. | [*wavy rule*] | LITTLE MATTIE.'; 5 'FALSE STEP.'; 7 'VOID IN LAW.'; 11 'LORD WALTER'S WIFE.'; 17 'BIANCA AMONG THE NIGHTINGALES.'; 24 'MY KATE.'; 26 'A SONG | FOR | THE RAGGED SCHOOLS OF LONDON.'; 33 'MAY'S LOVE.'; 34 'AMY'S CRUELTY.'; 37 'MY HEART AND I.'; 40 'THE BEST THING IN THE WORLD.'; 41 'WHERE'S AGNES?'; 48 'DE PROFUNDIS.'; 55 'A MUSICAL INSTRUMENT.'; 57 'FIRST NEWS FROM VILLAFRANCA.'; 59 'KING VICTOR EMANUEL ENTERING | FLORENCE, APRIL, 1860.'; 62 'THE SWORD OF CASTRUCCIO CASTRA-CANI.'; 65 'SUMMING UP IN ITALY. | (INSCRIBED TO IN-TELLIGENT PUBLICS OUT OF IT.)'; 69 ' "DIED . . ." | (*The 'Times' Obituary*.)'; 72 'THE FORCED RECRUIT. | SOLOFE-RINO, 1859.'; 75 'GARIBALDI.'; 78 'ONLY A CURL.'; 82 'A VIEW ACROSS THE ROMAN CAMPAGNA. | 1861.'; 85 'THE KING'S GIFT.'; 87 'PARTING LOVERS. | SIENA, 1860.'; 91 'MOTHER AND POET. | TURIN, AFTER NEWS FROM GAETA, 1861.'; 97 'NATURE'S REMORSES. | ROME, 1861.'; 101 'THE NORTH AND THE SOUTH. | [THE LAST POEM.] | ROME, MAY, 1861.'; 103 fly title 'TRANSLATIONS.'; [104] blank; 105 'PARAPHRASE ON THEOCRITUS. | [*french rule*] | THE CYCLOPS.'; 109 'PARAPHRASES ON APULEIUS. | [*french rule*] | PSYCHE GAZING ON CUPID.'; 111 'PSYCHE WAFTED BY ZEPHYRUS.'; 112 'PSYCHE AND PAN.'; 113 'PSYCHE PRO-PITIATING CERES.'; 115 'PSYCHE AND THE EAGLE.'; 116 'PSYCHE AND CERBERUS.'; 117 'PSYCHE AND PROSER-PINE.'; 118 'PSYCHE AND VENUS.'; 'MERCURY CARRIES PSYCHE TO OLYMPUS.'; 119 'MARRIAGE OF PSYCHE AND CUPID.'; 121 'PARAPHRASES ON NONNUS. | [*french rule*] |

HOW BACCHUS FINDS ARIADNE SLEEPING.'; 124 'HOW
BACCHUS COMFORTS ARIADNE.'; 126 'PARAPHRASE ON
HESIOD. | [french rule] | BACCHUS AND ARIADNE.'; 127
'PARAPHRASE ON EURIPIDES. | [french rule] | ANTI-
STROPE. | (TROADES, 853.*)'; 128 'PARAPHRASES ON
HOMER. | [french rule] | HECTOR AND ANDROMACHE.';
132 'THE DAUGHTERS OF PANDARUS.'; 135 'PARAPHRASE
ON ANACREON. | [french rule] | ODE TO THE SWALLOW.';
137 'PARAPHRASES ON HEINE. | [french rule] | [THE LAST
TRANSLATION] | ROME, 1860.'; 142 printer's imprint; [143]
advertisement for three titles headed 'WORKS | BY | ELIZA-
BETH BARRETT BROWNING' to 'POEMS BEFORE CON-
GRESS.'; [144] advertisement for three titles headed 'WORKS
BY ROBERT BROWNING' to 'CHRISTMAS EVE AND EAST-
ER DAY.'

Typography and paper: $1,2(-b2,K2) signed toward outer margin
of foot. Running titles set in rom. caps. with the titles of the individual works as 'GARIBALDI.' R.T. on p. 61 reads 'KING VIC-
TOR EMANUEL ENTE RING FLORENCE.' Pagination set in
the outer margin of the headline except pages 5, 7, 11, 17, 24, 33,
34, 37, 40, 41, 48, 55, 57, 59, 62, 65, 69, 72, 75, 78, 82, 85, 87, 91, 97,
101, 105, 109, 121, 127, 128, 135, 137 which are centered at the top.
Text irregular, 30 lines + headline and direction line. Leaf Kl^r
type page measures 14.1 (15.2) × 8.4 cm. Gutter margins measure
pp. 40–41 = 6.4 cm; 72–73 = 5.9 cm; 88–89 = 5.3 cm. White wove
paper unwatermarked. Sheets bulk 1.1 cm.

Binding: Violet pebble grain (P) cloth. Sides blind stamped with
a frame of three rules enclosing a boxed arabesque design with
corner and side ornaments. Spine: '[a series of rules and design of
leaves] | LAST | POEMS | [rule] | ELIZ. B. | BROWNING. |
[ornament] | CHAPMAN & HALL | [a series of rules and design
of leaves]'. All in gilt. The distance from the top of the publisher's
imprint to the bottom of the last rule on the spine measures 2.1 cm.
Brown coated end papers. Four stab holes at innner margin. Top
and fore edges unopened; bottom edge untrimmed.

Binding variant: As described but the distance indicated on the
spine measures 2.3 cm. (TxWB)

Notes: Published March 20, 1862 at six shillings. According to the
advertisement on page [vii] written by Robert Browning "these
poems are given as they ocur on a list drawn up last June [1861]."

Two impressions

A. As described with the following points: On page 33 the distance
from the inner type margin to the midpoint of the french rule is

exactly 2.4 cm. Line 13, page 39 reads ". . . by!" On page 55 the distance from the inner type margin to the midpoint of the french rule measures 3.1 cm. On line 20, page 91 the exclamation mark is under the letter a in the word "babes" of line 19. (TxU Wrenn)

B. As described with these variants: On page 33 the distance from the inner type margin to the midpoint of the french rule is 2.4+ cm. Line 13, page 39 reads ". . . by." On page 55 the distance from the inner type margin to the midpoint of the french rule measures 3.2+ cm. All of line 20, page 91 has been reset and the exclamation mark now appears midway between the letters a and b underneath the word "babes" of line 19. (TxU Stark)

The width of several type pages in the two impressions is as follows:

Page line	A	B
23.13	7.3+	7.3
50.22	5.6+	5.6
83.17	7.5	7.4

Copies examined: MH MB MWelC NN CtY IU TxU TxWB L O IaU CSmH CLU–C.

A14 : The Greek Christian Poets 1863

THE | GREEK CHRISTIAN POETS | AND THE | ENGLISH POETS. | BY | ELIZABETH BARRETT BROWNING. | LONDON: | CHAPMAN & HALL, 193, PICCADILLY. | 1863.

Special imprints: (p. [ii] in the center) PRINTED BY | JOHN EDWARD TAYLOR, LITTLE QUEEN STREET, | LINCOLN'S INN FIELDS. (p. 211 at the foot) JOHN EDWARD TAYLOR, PRINTER, | LITTLE QUEEN STREET, LINCOLN'S INN FIELDS.

Collation: 17.1 × 10.7 cm; [A]² B–O⁸ P²; 108 leaves.

Pagination: [i–iii] iv, [1] 2–103 [104] 105–211 [212].

Contents: [i] title page; [ii] printer's imprint; [iii] 'ADVERTISEMENT.' signed 'London, February, 1863.'; [1] 'SOME ACCOUNT OF THE GREEK | CHRISTIAN POETS.'; [104] blank; 105 'THE BOOK OF THE POETS.'; 211 'THE END.', printer's imprint; [212] advertisement for four titles headed 'WORKS | BY | ELIZABETH BARRETT BROWNING.' to 'LAST POEMS.'

Typography and paper: $1 signed toward outer margin of foot. Running titles set in rom. caps. as 'THE GREEK CHRISTIAN POETS.' Pagination set in outer margin of the headline except page 105 which is centered. Text 25 lines + headline and direction line.

Leaf II^r type page measures 12.6 (13.7) × 7.2 cm. Gutter margins measure, pp. 8–9 = 2.8 cm; 120–121 = 2.9 cm; 210–211 = 3.2 cm. On page 175 the number 1 is heavily damaged. White wove paper, unwatermarked. Sheets bulk 1.4 cm.

Binding: Green morocco (LI) cloth. Sides blind stamped with a border of three rules and corner ornaments. Spine: '[*rule*] | [*thick and thin rule*] | THE GREEK | CHRISTIAN | POETS | AND THE | ENGLISH | POETS | [*short rule*] | ELIZ. B | BROWNING | CHAPMAN & HALL | [*thin and thick rule*] | [*rule*]'. All in gilt. Brown coated end papers. Four stab holes at inner margin. Top and fore edges unopened; bottom edge untrimmed.

Binding variants: Purple sand grain (C) cloth. Sides blind stamped with two rules enclosing a floral design. Spine: '[*two rules*] | THE | GREEK | CHRISTIAN | POETS. | [*short rule*] | BROWNING. | [*emblem*] | [*two rules*]'. Rules at head and foot of spine stamped in blind; lettering and short rule in gilt. Yellow coated end papers. (TxWB)

Green sand grain (C) cloth. Sides blind stamped with an ornate decorated rule. Spine: '[*series of five rules*] | BROWNING'S | GREEK | CHRISTIAN | POETS | ETC. | [*ornament*] | [*series of six rules*]'. All in gilt. Cream coated end papers. (TxU)

Notes: Published March 9, 1863 at five shillings. E.B.B. had published the essays in the *Athenaeum* in 1842 and had made certain revisions to the text anticipating their publication in book form prior to her death.

Four states

A. As described with the following points: Lines 16–17 page 205 read '. . . all
   '. . . full (NIC)
B. As described with this variant: Lines 16–17 page 205 read '. . . al
   '. . . full (TxU)
C. As described with this variant. Lines 16–17 page 205 read '. . . all
   '. . . ful (CtY)
D. †As described with this variant: Lines 16–17 page 205 read '. . . al
   '. . . ful (0)
†note: a copy at the Huntington Library exhibits an intermediate state with the second letter l in the word 'all' barely visible.

Copies examined: NIC NN DLC MH MB MWelC IU ICN TxU TxWB L O CLU–C CSmH IaU.

FUGITIVE PRINTINGS
AND FORGERIES

B : POSTHUMOUSLY PRINTED WORKS

AND THE FORGERIES OF WISE

AND HIS CONFEDERATES

B1 : **The Runaway Slave at Pilgrim's Point** [1888]

First impression

[*within a frame of two rules*] THE | RUNAWAY SLAVE | AT
PILGRIM'S POINT. | BY | ELIZABETH BARRETT BROWN-
ING. | [*floral ornament*] | LONDON: | CHAPMAN & HALL, 193
PICCADILLY. | 1849.

Collation: 20.0 × 14.2 cm; [Unsigned 1^{12} (1_{7+1})]; 13 leaves.

Special imprint: (p. [26] at the center) LONDON: | BRADBURY
AND EVANS, Printers, WHITEFRIARS.

Pagination: [1–7] 8–24 [25–26].

Contents: [1] half title 'THE RUNAWAY SLAVE'; [2] blank; [3]
title page; [4] blank; [5] 'ADVERTISEMENT.' signed 'FLOR-
ENCE, 1849.'; [6] blank; [7] text; [25] blank; [26] printer's imprint.

Typography and paper: Unsigned. Running titles set in rom. caps.
over a single rule. Versos read 'THE RUNAWAY SLAVE'; rectos
read 'AT PILGRIM'S POINT.' Pagination set in the outer margin
of the headline. Each page enclosed by a ruled frame 14.5 × 8.6
cm. Printed on a semi-stiff wove cream paper. Sheets bulk 0.2 cm.

Binding: Tan paper wrappers with typography of title page reproduced on front. Back wrapper blank. Three stab holes at inner
margin. All edges trimmed.

Copies examined: TxU, Alexander Trumbull Library Copy
(photostat)

Second impression

[*within a frame of two rules*] THE | RUNAWAY SLAVE | AT
PILGRIM'S POINT. | BY | ELIZABETH BARRETT BROWN-
ING. | [*ornament of two birds and serpent*] | LONDON: | ED-
WARD MOXON, DOVER STREET. | 1849.

Special imprint: (p. [27] at the center) LONDON: | BRADBURY
AND EVANS, PRINTERS, WHITEFRIARS.

Collation: 20.6 × 13.9 cm; [unsigned $1-3^4$ 4^2]; 14 leaves.

Pagination: [1–9] 10–26 [27–28].

Contents: 1 blank leaf; [3] half title 'THE RUNAWAY SLAVE.';
[4] blank; [5] title page; [6] blank; [7] 'ADVERTISEMENT.'
dated 'FLORENCE, 1849.'; [8] blank; [9] text; [27] printer's imprint; [28] blank.

Typography and paper: Unsigned with the typographical features of the first impression. All gutter margins measure 4.7 cm. Printed on stiff wove cream paper. Sheets bulk 0.3 cm.

Binding: Cream colored wrappers, with typography of title page reproduced on front. Back wrapper blank. Two stab holes at inner margin. All edges trimmed. Single binder's leaf at front and back.

Notes: This pamphlet, perhaps the most infamous of Thomas J. Wise's forgeries, was proven fraudulent through John Carter's and Graham Pollard's investigation in 1934. The paper was found to be composed of chemical wood fibre with a trace of rag which could not have been manufactured before 1874, and more likely after 1883. The type, a small pica, "modern style" designated Type B was not manufactured for the firm of Richard Clay and Sons who printed the forgery before 1880.

A comparison of the Chapman and Hall and Moxon pamphlets on the Hinman collator reveals that there were two distinct impressions, not merely a corrected state as previously noted. The textual variants are as follows: (Roman numerals refer to stanza numbers; arabic numbers to lines:)

	CHAPMAN & HALL	EDWARD MOXON
I.5	night, ...	night— ...
	dark;	dark—
II.7	Who in your names	Who, in your names,
IV.4	he	He
.5	his	His
VI.4	prison bars:	prison-bars!
.7	the prison-bars	their prison bars
VIII.2	But ... glee,	And ... glee;
.3	colour	color
.6	slave ... slave	Slave ... Slave
IX.6	mind,	mind;
.7	freedom	liberty
X.1	sunny ground	open ground,
.4	fast:	fast.
.5	smiled	sate
.6	As ... cocoa-nut	And ... cocoa-nut,
XI.3	along	along,
.6	guess	guess,
XIII.2	bliss,	bliss;
	XV	Xv
XVI.1	low, low	low-low-
.3	babe	babe,
XVII.7	master-right.	master's right.

XX.2 1	I
XXI.3 lay instead	lay, instead,
.5 cold	cold—
XXIV.7 his	His
XXVI.1 was all	all was
XXVII.3 it, soft	it,—soft
XXVIII.3 free	great
XXIX.1 hunter sons	hunter-sons
.2 me—	me!
.3 off! . . . once!	off—. . . once!—
XXX.7 likes the	liketh
XXXI.6 wrist	wrist,
XXXIII.5 fair,	fair;
XXXIV.3 Christs	Christ's

Not only do the two pamphlets have a different imposition plus the above textual changes, but more than half of the lines of every page have been reset. Each headline also is reset, the text of the first impression extending from page [7]–24; the second impression extending from page [9]–26.

A collation of the poem's first appearance in the *Liberty Bell* (Boston, 1848) with the *Poems* of 1850, 1853, 1856, 1862, and 1864, with the two forgeries reveals a total of 42 substantive changes. The collation shows that Wise did not print the Chapman and Hall pamphlet from a late edition of the *Poems*, as formerly stated, but from the beginning he deliberately produced a forgery whose text was taken from both the *Liberty Bell* and a late edition of the *Poems*. (In the table below several examples are given. Roman numerals refer to the stanza of the forgeries; arabic numbers to lines:)

LIBERTY BELL	POEMS 1850	POEMS 1853
I.3 changed	turned	turned
III.7 heretofore	evermore	evermore
VII.1 How be it	And still	And still
VII.4 wold	fold	fold
XI.5 But I sang	I sang	I sang
XI.6 what	aught	aught
XII.3 on Thee	to Thee	to Thee
XIV.1 greater	deeper	deeper
XXXII.3 grace	joy	joy

POEMS 1856*	CHAPMAN & HALL	EDWARD MOXON
I.3 turned	changed	changed
III.7 evermore	heretofore	heretofore
VII.1 And still	How be it	How be it

VII.4 fold	wold	wold
XI.5 I sang	I sang	I sang
XI.6 aught	aught	aught
XII.3 to Thee	on Thee	on Thee
XIV.1 deeper	greater	greater
XXXII.3 joy	joy	joy

* The editions of Poems of 1862 and 1864 give similar readings.

After the Chapman and Hall pamphlet had been printed, it no doubt occurred to Wise or one of his confederates that in 1849 E.B.B. was not using Chapman and Hall for a publisher, but Edward Moxon, and a second impression with the corrected imprint was struck. Many changes made to the poem here restore the text of the *Liberty Bell*, but as the above table shows in a number of instances the text of a late edition of the *Poems* was retained.

In a note in *The Book Collector*, XII (Spring 1963), 68-71, Mr. George Chapman Singer reported that the title leaf of his copy of *The Runaway Slave* contained a set off from page 67-68 of the 'NOTE BOOK OF THE SHELLEY SOCIETY'. In the Wrenn copy (1) at the University of Texas on leaf [A1r] there is a set off from an unidentified page the headline of which reads 'THE SHELLEY SOCIETY'. What appears to be the twelfth (?) line of text reads . . . "May 25, 1886." In Wrenn copy (2) there is another set off on leaves [A1v] and [A4r], the headline of which reads 'NOTEBOOK OF THE SHELLEY SOCIETY.' The Shelley Society Notebook was issued in 1888 and printed by the firm of Richard Clay & Son, and as Mr. Singer remarks the set offs constitute an indelible proof of the relationship between Wise's admitted connection with the Shelley Society's publications and the forgery of The Runaway Slave.

A holograph manuscript of the poem is at Baylor.

Copies examined: TxU TxWB IaU MWelC MH L O CSmH.

B2 : Sonnets, 1847 [*ca.* 1893]

SONNETS. | BY | E.B.B. | READING: | [NOT FOR PUBLICATION.] | [*short rule 0.5+ cm*] | 1847.

Special imprints: none.

Collation: 21.0 × 13.0 cm untrimmed; [A]⁸ B–C⁸; 24 leaves.

Pagination: [1–5] 6–47 [48].

Contents: [1] half title 'SONNETS.'; [2] blank; [3] title page; [4]

blank; [5] 'SONNETS. | I. | I THOUGHT once how Theocritus
had sung'; 6 'II. | But only three in all God's universe'; 7 'III. | Un-
like are we, unlike, O princely Heart!'; 8 'IV. | Thou hast thy
calling to some palace floor,'; 9 'V. | I lift my heavy heart up
solemnly,'; 10 'VI. | Go from me. Yet I feel that I shall stand'; 11
'VII. | The face of all the world is changed, I think,'; 12 'VIII. |
What can I give thee back, O liberal'; 13 'IX. | Can it be right to
give what I can give?'; 14 'X. | Yet love, mere love, is beautiful
indeed'; 15 'XI. | And therefore if to love can be desert,'; 16 'XII. |
Indeed this very love which is my boast,'; 17 'XIII. | And wilt thou
have me fashion into speech'; 18 'XIV. | If thou must love me, let
it be for nought'; 19 'XV. | Accuse me not, beseech thee, that I
wear'; 20 'XVI. | And yet, because thou overcomest so,'; 21 'XVII. |
My poet, thou canst touch on all the notes'; 22 'XVIII. | I never
gave a lock of hair away'; 23 'XIX. | The soul's Rialto hath its
merchandise;'; 24 'XX | Beloved, my Beloved, when I think'; 25
'XXI. | Say over again and yet once over again'; 26 'XXII. | When
our two souls stand up erect and strong,'; 27 'XXIII. | Is it indeed
so? If I lay here dead'; 28 'XXIV. | Let the world's sharpness like
a clasping knife'; 29 'XXV. | A heavy heart, Beloved, have I borne';
30 'XXVI. | I lived with visions for my company'; 31 'XXVII. | My
own Beloved, who has lifted me'; 32 'XXVIII. | My letters! all dead
paper, . . . mute and white!—'; 33 'XXIX. | I think of thee!—my
thoughts do twine and bud'; 34 'XXX. | I see thine image through
my tears to-night,'; 35 'XXXI. | Thou comest! all is said without a
word.'; 36 'XXXII. | The first time that the sun rose on thine oath';
37 'XXXIII. | Yes, call me by my pet-name! let me hear'; 38
'XXXIV. | With the same heart, I said, I'll answer thee'; 39 XXXV
'If I leave all for thee, wilt thou exchange'; 40 'XXXXVI. | When
we met first and loved, I did not build'; 41 XXXVII. | Pardon, oh,
pardon, that my soul should make'; 42 'XXXVIII. | First time he
kissed me, he but only kissed'; 43 'XXXIX. | Because thou hast the
power and own'st the grace'; 44 'XL. | Oh, yes! they love through
all this world of ours!'; 45 'XLI. | I thank all who have loved me in
their hearts,'; 46 'XLII. | How do I love thee? Let me count the
ways.'; 47 'XLIII. |Beloved, thou hast brought me many flowers';
[48] blank.

Typography and paper: $1,2 signed toward outer margin of foot.
Running titles set in rom. caps. as 'SONNETS.'. Pagination set in
the outer margin of the headline. Text 15 lines + headline and
direction line. Leaf B2ʳ type page measures 10.0 (11.9) × 7.9 cm.
Gutter margins measure pp. 8–9 = 2.7 cm; 24–25 = 2.6 cm; 40–
41 = 2.7 cm. There is no period after roman numeral XX on page
24. White wove paper unwatermarked. Sheets bulk 0.3 cm.

Binding: According to Wise the pamphlet was issued stitched without wrappers, but almost all copies extant are rebound; probably they were on Wise's order rebound at the time of issue. One copy unbound is at Harvard.

Notes: This edition of the sonnets was revealed as a forgery attributed to Thomas J. Wise and others through an examination of the book's paper and typography by John Carter and Graham Pollard in 1934. Their research indicated the paper to be comprised of chemical wood with a trace of rag, which could not have been manufactured before 1874, and was unlikely before 1883. Printed in Clay's Long Primer No. 3 of which certain letters were not cut until after 1880. Probable printing about 21 June 1893 on evidence of a letter of the date from Gosse to Wise.
Textual variants between the forgery and the actual first appearance of the sonnets in *Poems*, 1850 are as follows:

Sonnet.line	1847	1850
V.10	They	Thou
XXIII.10	look..	look on me..
	breathe on me	breathe on me!
XXXIV.14	can run	could run
XXXVI.14	star fore fold	star foretold

Manuscripts of the Sonnets are held at the British Museum, the Pierpont Morgan Library, and the Library of Arthur A. Houghton, Jr. A variorum edition with transcriptions from the three manuscripts was published by P. C. Duschnes in 1950 (D 350). It does not contain the textual variants in the editions of 1850 and 1853 however.

Copies examined: TxU MWelC IaU MH CLU–C CSmH.

B3 : Religious Opinions 1896

THE | RELIGIOUS OPINIONS | OF | ELIZABETH BARRETT | BROWNING | AS EXPRESSED IN THREE LETTERS TO | WM. MERRY, ESQ., J.P. | *Edited by the Rev.* | *W. Robertson Nicoll, L.L.D.* | LONDON: | PRIVATELY PRINTED. | 1896.

Special imprint: (p. [29] at the center) device of the Ashley Library.

Collation: 21.1 × 15.1 cm; [Unsigned $1^4 2^8 3^4$]; 16 leaves.

Pagination: [2] [1–7] 8 [9–11] 12–28 [29–30].

Contents: 1 blank leaf; [1] half title 'THE RELIGIOUS OPIN-
IONS | OF | ELIZABETH BARRETT BROWNING'; [2] blank;
[3] title page; [4] blank; [5] 'This is to certify | that of this book |
Thirty Copies only have been printed.'; [6] blank; [7] editor's
preface; [9] fly title 'LETTERS.'; [10] blank; [11] 'LETTER I. |
[*rule*] | 50 WIMPOLE STREET, | LONDON. | *November 2nd,*
1843.'; 18 'LETTER II. | [*rule*] | 50 WIMPOLE STREET, | LON-
DON. | *November 17th,* 1843.'; [29] device of the Ashley Library;
[30] blank.

Typography and paper: Unsigned. Running titles set in italic caps
on versos as 'THE RELIGIOUS OPINIONS OF' and on rectos as
'ELIZABETH BARRETT BROWNING.'. Pagination set in the
outer margin of the headline. Text 30 lines + headline. Leaf [2_4^r]
type page measures 14.1 (14.8) × 9.3 cm. Gutter margins measure,
pp. 14–15 = 4.3 cm; 26–27 = 4.3 cm. White laid paper, unwatermarked; chain lines 2.6 cm. apart. Sheets bulk 0.2 cm.

Binding: White paper boards. Sides blank. Running up the spine
'THE RELIGIOUS OPINIONS OF E. B. BROWNING'. All in
gilt. White laid end papers. Four stab holes at inner margin. Top
and fore edges unopened; bottom edge trimmed.

Notes: The editor's introduction states that E.B.B.'s letters to Mr.
Merry were written in response to his sending her a copy of his recently published book, *Predestination and Election, Considered
Spiritually*, London, 1843. As such, they touch on a rather small
aspect of the author's religious opinions, and in no way constitute
a summation ever intended for publication. In a footnote the editor acknowledges his gratitude to Robert Wiedemann Barrett
Browning for permission to publish the letters.
Examination on the Hinman collator of this book with pages 121–
142 of *Literary Anecdotes of the Nineteenth Century*, edited by
W. Robertson Nicoll and Thomas J. Wise (London 1896) shows
that there were two settings of type, but the format, paper, and
type of the former are an almost identical duplication of the latter.
Copies examined: TxU TxWB MWelC MH L O.

B4 : A Song 1907

A Song | *BY* | *ELIZABETH BARRETT BROWNING* | [*short rule
1.3+ cm*] | *Privately printed* | [*short rule 1.3+ cm.*] | *1907.*

Collation: 16.8 × 10.7 cm; [A]²; 2 leaves.

Pagination: [1–3] 4.

Contents: [1] title page; [2] blank; [3] 'A SONG | [*ornamental rule]* | I ⟨first line reads:⟩ Is't loving, to list to the night guitar,'; 4 'II | ⟨first line reads:⟩ Unless you can think when the song is done,', signed E.B.B. at the foot.

Typography and paper: Unsigned. A single sheet folded once, probably imposed in half sheets. Running title on page 4 only set in italic caps as 'A SONG' and printed over a single rule. The only numbered page set in italic in the outer margin of the headline. Text irregular, 9 lines + headline. Leaf [A2ᵛ] measures 6.0 (9.2) × 6.8+ cm. White laid paper unwatermarked. Chain lines set 2.6 cm apart.

Notes: There is no indication either in the pamphlet or in Thomas J. Wise's bibliography to attribute this piracy to him; a manuscript note written by George A. Aitken on one copy at The University of Texas reads "one of twenty copies printed by Thomas J. Wise."

Copies examined: TxU TxWB MWelC L O.

B5 : Leila 1913

LEILA | A TALE | BY | ELIZABETH BARRETT BROWNING | LONDON: | PRINTED FOR PRIVATE CIRCULATION ONLY | 1913.

Special imprint: (p. [36] at the center) LONDON: | Printed for THOMAS J. WISE, Hampstead, N.W. | *Edition limited to Thirty Copies.*

Collation: 19.2 × 12.7 cm; [A]¹⁸; 18 leaves.

Pagination: [1–7] 8–21 [22] 23–34 [36].

Contents: [1] half title 'LEILA | A TALE'; [2] blank; [3] title page; [4] 'NOTE.' signed 'T.J.W.'; [5] blank; [6] 'LEILA | A TALE | CANTO I.'; [22] 'CANTO II.'; [36] imprint.

Typography and paper: Leaves [A3ʳ] [A6ʳ] [A7ʳ] missigned B2 C C2 respectively. Running titles set in rom. caps. as 'LEILA: A TALE'. Pagination set in the outer margin of the headline. Text irregular, 25 lines + headline and direction line. Leaf [A6ʳ] type page measures 12.0 (13.1) × 7.6 cm. The single gutter margin, pp. 18–19 measures 3.4 cm. White wove paper, unwatermarked. Sheets bulk 0.3 cm.

Binding: Tan paper wrappers. On front typography identical to title page. Back wrapper blank. Two stab holes at inner margin. Top and fore edges unopened; bottom edge untrimmed.

Notes: According to Wise, the poem was composed by E.B.B. about the year 1830 and printed from a manuscript in his collection.

Copies examined: TxU MWelC L O.

B6 : The Enchantress 1913

THE ENCHANTRESS | AND OTHER POEMS | BY | ELIZA-BETH BARRETT BROWNING | LONDON: | PRINTED FOR PRIVATE CIRCULATION ONLY | 1913.

Special imprint: (p. [29] at the center) LONDON: | Printed for THOMAS J. WISE, Hampstead, N.W. | *Edition limited to Thirty Copies.*

Collation: 19.2 × 12.7 cm; [A]¹⁶; 16 leaves.

Pagination: [1–7] 8–11 [12] 13–18 [19–20] 21 [22] 23 [24] 25–26 [27] 28 [29–30] [2].

Contents: [1] half title 'THE ENCHANTRESS'; [2] blank; [3] title page; [4] blank; [5] 'CONTENTS'; [6] blank; [7] 'THE EN-CHANTRESS'; [12] 'A TRUE DREAM | (Dreamed at Sidmouth, 1833.)'; [19] 'TRANSLATION FROM | CLAUDIAN'; [20] 'A VISION'; [22] 'CLEODAMUS AND MYRSON | (*Translated from the Greek of Bion.*)'; [24] 'THOUGHTS AWAKENED BY CON- | TEMPLATING A PIECE OF THE PALM | WHICH GROWS ON THE | SUMMIT OF THE ATHENIAN | ACROPO-LIS'; [27] 'MARY MADDOX'; [29] imprint; [30] blank; 1 blank leaf.

Typography and paper: Leaves [A5ʳ] [A6ʳ] missigned B and B2 respectively. Running titles set in italic caps. as '*POEMS*'. Pagination set in the outer margin of the headline. Text irregular, 25 lines + headline and direction line. Leaf [A6ʳ] type page measures 12.1 (13.2) × 7.7 cm. The single gutter margin, pp. 16–17, measures 3.4 cm. White wove paper unwatermarked. Sheets bulk 0.2 cm.

Binding: Tan paper wrappers. On front typography identical to title page. Back wrapper blank. Two stab holes at inner margin. Top and fore edges unopened; bottom edge untrimmed.

Notes: Contents printed from manuscripts obtained in the Sotheby sale of 1913. Material reprinted on several occasions.

Copies examined: TxU MWelC L O.

B7 : **Epistle to a Canary 1913**

EPISTLE TO A CANARY | 1837 | BY | ELIZABETH BARRETT BARRETT | EDITED | BY | EDMUND GOSSE, C.B. | LONDON: | PRINTED FOR PRIVATE CIRCULATION ONLY | 1913.

Special imprint: (p. [20] at the center) 'LONDON: | Printed for THOMAS J. WISE, Hampstead, N.W. | Edition limited to Thirty Copies.

Collation: 19.2 × 12.6 cm; [A]¹⁰; 10 leaves.

Pagination: [1–6] 7 [8–9] 10–19 [20].

Contents: [1] half title 'EPISTLE TO A CANARY'; [2] blank; [3] title page; [4] blank; [5] 'INTRODUCTION' signed EDMUND GOSSE.' and dated *June*, 1913.' [8] 'Note.' signed 'T.J.W.'; [9] text; [20] imprint.

Typography and paper: Unsigned. Running titles set in rom caps. as 'EPISTLE TO A CANARY'. Pagination set in the outer margin of the headline. Text irregular, 26 lines + headline. Leaf [A7ʳ] type page measures 12.1 (12.7) × 7.7 cm. The single gutter margin, pp. 10–11, measures 3.4 cm. White wove paper, unwatermarked. Sheets bulk 0.1+ cm.

Binding: Tan paper wrappers. On front typography identical to title page. Back wrapper blank. Two stab holes at inner margin. Top and fore edges unopened; bottom edge untrimmed.

Notes: The manuscript of this poem was the property of Edmund Gosse. According to his introduction, he believes the poem was written by E.B.B. in 1837 in reference to the pet canary owned by Mary Russell Mitford.

Copies examined: TxU MWelC L O.

B8 : **The Poet's Enchiridion 1914**

[*in red*] THE | POETS' ENCHIRIDION | [*in black*] A HITHERTO UNPUBLISHED POEM | WITH AN INEDITED | ADDRESS TO UVEDALE PRICE | ON HIS EIGHTIETH BIRTHDAY | AN EARLY | INVOCATION TO SLEEP | AND A PRELIMINARY DRAFT OF | THE RENOWNED POEM | CATARINA TO CAMOENS | BY | ELIZABETH BARRETT BARRETT | (AFTERWARDS MRS. BROWNING) | [*in blue*,

seal of the Bibliophile Society] | [*in black*] PRINTED EXCLU-
SIVELY FOR MEMBERS OF | [*in red*] THE BIBLIOPHILE
SOCIETY | [*in black*] BOSTON, MASSACHUSETTS |
MCMXIV

Special imprints: none.

Collation: 23.1 × 16.5 cm; [unsigned $1^{10}(-1_1)$ 2–4^8]; 33 leaves.

Pagination: [6], [1–4] 5–6 [7–8] 9–34 [35–36] 37–43 [44] 45–49
[50] 51–53 [54] [6].

Contents: 3 blank leaves; [1] half title 'THE POETS' ENCHIR-
IDION | ADDRESS TO UVEDALE PRICE | AN INVOCATION
TO SLEEP | CATARINA TO CAMOENS'; [2] blank; [3] title
page; [4] 'COPYRIGHT, 1914, BY | THE BIBLIOPHILE SO-
CIETY'; 5 'NOTE'; [7] fly title 'ELIZABETH BARRETT
BROWNING' : | NEW DATA'; [8] blank; 9 text; 19 'Oh! thou!
whom Fortune led to stray', 'Sweet Parent! dear to me as kind'; 20
'SUMMER'; 21 'AURORA', 'TO SUMMER'; 23 'ON PAPA'S
BIRTHDAY: MAY 28TH, 1815'; 25 'ON THE CLOCK PUT UP
AT HOPE END— | MAY, 1815'; 28 'MY EVER EVER DEAREST
PUPPY,'; [35] fly title 'THE POETS' ENCHIRIDION | ADDRESS
TO UVEDALE PRICE | AN INVOCATION TO SLEEP | CATA-
RINA TO CAMOENS'; [36] blank; 37 'THE POETS' ENCHIR-
IDION'; 41 'TO UVEDALE PRICE, ESQr. | *On his birthday,
March 26, 1827*'; [44] blank; 45 'BEFORE SLEEPING | *An In-
vocation*'; 47 'CATARINA TO CAMOENS | *An Early Draft*'; [50]
blank; 51 'TO LAURA BUXTON FORMAN' ⟨text of a poem
about E.B.B. by H. Buxton Forman⟩; [54] blank; 3 blank leaves.

Typography and paper: unsigned. Leaf [1₁] pasted under the
front end paper. Leaves [1₂] and [4₃] used as pastedowns. No
headlines are present. Pagination centered at the bottom of the
page. Text irregular, 29 lines + direction line. Leaf [2₁ʳ] measures
13.2 (13.7) × 8.5 cm. Gutter margins measure; pp. 20–21 = 6.0
cm; 52–53 = 5.2 cm; White wove paper watermarked 'VAN
GELDER HOLLAND BIBLIOPHILE SOCIETY'. Sheets bulk
0.8 cm.

Binding: Tan cloth with velum backstrip. At the center of front
cover stamped in gilt 'ELIZABETH BARRETT BROWNING.'
Back and spine entirely blank. Boxed. Ten stab holes at inner
margin. Top edge gilt; fore edge unopened; bottom edge trimmed.

Notes: Published by the Bibliophile Society, Boston, in 1914 for its
members "as a foretaste of the unusual literary treat that awaits
them in the two larger volumes of unpublished Browning MSS.

[*Hitherto unpublished Poems and Stories*] now in course of preparation." The edition consisted of 500 copies and sold at $4.50. The book was edited by Harry Buxton Forman from the Barrett-Browning papers obtained in the Sotheby sale of 1913 by Henry H. Harper, who, according to Forman, "placed [the manuscripts] at the disposal of the Society to print for the members."

Copies examined: TxWB TxU MB MWelC L.

B9 : Hitherto Unpublished Poems 1914

[*within an elaborate ornamental frame*] ELIZABETH BARRETT | BROWNING | HITHERTO UNPUBLISHED | POEMS AND STORIES | WITH AN INEDITED | AUTOBIOGRAPHY | [*ornament*] | PRINTED EXCLUSIVELY FOR | MEMBERS OF | [*ornament*] THE [*ornament*] | BIBLIOPHILE SOCIETY | BOSTON—MCMXIV.

Special imprints: Vol. 1 (p. [174] at the center) device of the DE VINNE PRESS. Vol. 2 (p. [244] at the center) device of the DE VINNE PRESS.

Collation: Vol. 1 22.8 × 16.0 cm; [unsigned 1–3⁸ 4⁶ 5–15⁸]; 118 leaves + 4 plates. Vol. 2 22.8 × 16.0 cm; [unsigned 1–14⁸ 15¹⁰]; 122 leaves + 4 plates.

Pagination: Vol. 1 [2] [i–ii], [vii–viii], ix–lxii [= lviii], [1–2] 3–28 [29–30] 31–162 [163–164] 165–173 [174] [2]. Vol. 2 [1–2] 3–243 [244].

Contents: Vol. 1 1 blank leaf; [i] half title 'ELIZABETH BAR-RETT BROWNING'; [ii] blank; [vii] 'NOTE'; [viii] blank; ix 'INTRODUCTION | BY H. BUXTON FORMAN, C.B.' signed by H.B.F. and dated '28 October, 1914.'; [1] fly title 'GLIMPSES INTO MY OWN LIFE AND | LITERARY CHARACTER | [*short rule*] | WRITTEN BY ELIZABETH BARRETT | IN THE YEAR 1820 | WHEN FOURTEEN YEARS OLD'; [2] blank; 3 text; [29] fly title 'EARLY VERSE AND PROSE FROM | THE HOPE END ARCHIVES'; [30] blank; 31 ⟨1⟩ 'ON THE CRUELTY OF FORCEMENT TO MAN; | ALLUDING TO THE PRESS GANG', ⟨2⟩ 'ON EARLY RISING'; 32 ⟨3⟩ 'Ye lovely lillies of the Vale', ⟨4⟩ 'Near to a shady wood where Fir trees grew'; 33 ⟨5⟩ 'Ah! Virture, come my steps to stay', ⟨6⟩ 'Loft on the top of that high hill a lonely cottage/stood', ⟨7⟩ 'Upon the boundaries of a lofty Wood'; 34 ⟨8⟩ 'Oh! thou! whom Fortune led to stray', ⟨9⟩ 'Soft as the dew from Heaven descends'; 35 ⟨10⟩ 'Soft

were the murmurs of the gentle rill,', ⟨11⟩ 'As I was walking by a
hedge, . . .'; 36 ⟨12⟩ 'TO MY DEAREST PAPA!'; 37 ⟨13⟩ 'ON
THE RETURN OF THE FINE SEASON— | APRIL 29', ⟨14⟩
'OCCASIONED BY A FALL OF SNOW, MAY 6—1814'; 38
⟨15⟩ 'IN IMITATION OF "PITY THE SORROWS OF | A POOR
OLD MAN"', ⟨16⟩ 'SENT TO MAMA ON 1ST MAY, 1814'; 39
⟨17⟩ 'THE HERMIT'; 40 ⟨18⟩ 'TO FLORA—7TH MAY, 1814',
⟨19⟩ 'ON AN ERUPTION OF MOUNT ETNA: | 8TH MAY,
1814'; 41 ⟨20⟩ 'TO THE FISHING NET.—WRITTEN THE
MORNING | THE POND WAS DRAWN AT HOPE END, |
10TH MAY 1814', ⟨21⟩ 'Mine's the sweet home in yonder cell'; 42
⟨22⟩ 'AN EPISTLE TO HENRIETTA'; 43 ⟨23⟩ 'Wild were the
windings of the stream'; 44 ⟨24⟩ 'ADDRESSED TO DEAREST
PAPA ON HIS BIRTHDAY, | UPON THE RECOVERY OF
LITTLE ARABELLA | FROM A DANGEROUS ILLNESS'; 45
⟨25⟩ 'UPON THE ROSE BLOWING AFTER THE LILLY— |
CARLTON—JUNE 8TH, 1814', ⟨26⟩ 'Oh! Virtue's gone, sweet
Virtue flies,'; 46 ⟨27⟩ 'ON VISITING MATLOCK, DERBY-
SHIRE'; 48 ⟨28⟩ 'TO HER UNCLE SAM, WITH HER POETRY,';
⟨29⟩ 'A SONG'; 49 ⟨30⟩ 'ON FIRST SEEING THE SEA AT
TYNEMOUTH'; 51 ⟨31⟩ 'THE BEGGAR BOY'S PETITION TO
LITTLE SAM', ⟨32⟩ 'Fair Emma pluckt the sweet carnation,'; 52
⟨33⟩ 'ON A SHIP BEING LOST AT TYNEMOUTH | LINES
WRITTEN AT FENHAM, 4TH AUGUST, 1814'; 53 ⟨34⟩ 'Ah!
now, stern winter's chilling blast returns,' ⟨35⟩ 'AN EPISTLE TO
DEAREST PAPA IN LONDON'; 55 ⟨36⟩ 'Down in a Vale, a little
cottage stood,'; 56 ⟨37⟩ 'Fair and chrystal is the Spring,'; 57 ⟨38⟩
'PROLOGUE'; 59 ⟨39⟩ 'ON HEARING CATALANI SING, AND
BEING TOLD | HER STORY'; 61 ⟨40⟩ 'AFTER A SHOWER OF
RAIN—TO MAMA; HOPE END, | 3RD OCTOBER, 1814'; ⟨41⟩
'FIRST FRENCH LINES—HOPE END, | OCTOBER 25, 1814';
62 ⟨42⟩ 'SEBASTIAN, OR THE LOST CHILD—A TALE | OF
OTHER TIMES'; 65 ⟨43⟩ 'DISOBEDIENCE'; 68 ⟨44⟩ '"THE
WAY TO HUMBLE PRIDE"'; 72 ⟨45⟩ 'Oh! Virtue sweet, Oh!
beauteous Truth,', ⟨46⟩ 'Far along a rugged wood'; 73 ⟨47⟩ 'By a
large and spacious plain,'; 74 ⟨48⟩ 'HANNIBAL'S PASSAGE OF
THE ALPS'; 76 ⟨49⟩ 'By the side of a hill hollow', ⟨50⟩ 'As I wan-
dered along thro' a Wood,'; 77 ⟨51⟩ 'Down in a Vale a cottage
rose,'; 78 ⟨52⟩ 'In a Vale a lilly droops,', ⟨53⟩ 'THE SEASONS.—
HOPE END, 12TH NOVEMBER, 1814— | JANUARY, 1815'; 80
⟨54⟩ 'TO LITTLE SAM ON HIS BIRTHDAY—HOPE END, |
13TH JAN'Y, 1815'; 81 ⟨55⟩ 'AURORA'; 82 ⟨56⟩ 'ON MR. BELL'S
SICKNESS AT HOPE END— | MARCH, 1815'; 83 ⟨57⟩ 'TO
MAMA—HOPE END, 23RD MARCH, 1815'; 84 ⟨58⟩ 'A King is a
Man, the same as a Beggar; . . .', ⟨59⟩ 'OF PROPHECY'; 85 ⟨60⟩

'AN ADDRESS TO TRUTH'; 86 ⟨61⟩ 'Amid the secret windings of a grove', ⟨62⟩ 'ON THE FIRST OF MAY—MAMA'S BIRTH-DAY— 1815'; 87 ⟨63⟩ 'ON THE CLOCK PUT UP AT HOPE END—MAY, 1815'; 88 ⟨64⟩ 'ON PAPA'S BIRTHDAY: MAY 28TH, 1815'; 91 ⟨65⟩ 'ON MORNING'; 92 ⟨66⟩ 'Where can happiness be found?'; 94 ⟨67⟩ 'TO SUMMER'; 95 ⟨68⟩ 'TO THE MUSE', ⟨69⟩ 'ON POVERTY'; 96 ⟨70⟩ 'TO FLORA'; 97 ⟨71⟩ 'See that rock which o'er looks the turbulent deep,'; ⟨72⟩ 'TO EVENING'; 98 ⟨73⟩ 'ON A ROSE PULLED ON A DEWEY MORNING'; 99 ⟨74⟩ 'TO DEAREST HENRIETTA ON HER BIRTHDAY | AT BREAKFAST, | WITH WISHES FOR HER GOOD APPETITE'; 100 ⟨75⟩ 'Come forth thou blessed strain of poetry,'; 101 ⟨76⟩ 'Look up that mountain's craggy steep,', ⟨77⟩ 'TO MY DEAREST PAPA—ON HIS BIRTHDAY'; 103 ⟨78⟩ 'Accept my gift! for love's sweet couch is flowers,'; ⟨79⟩ 'May flowery gales, which waft this pledge of love,'; 104 ⟨80⟩ 'THE CATHEDRAL'; 105 ⟨81⟩ 'TO PAPA AND MAMA!'; 106 ⟨82⟩ 'Soyez satisfaite, O génération d'Adam!'; 108 ⟨83⟩ 'TO MY DEAREST BROTHER EDWARD | (ON HIS BIRTHDAY) | HOPE END, JUNE 26, 1816'; 109 ⟨84⟩ 'MORNING—NOVEMBER, 1816'; 110 ⟨85⟩ 'REGULUS'; 122 ⟨86⟩ 'AFTER THE FARCE OF HAMLET, THE EPILOGUE | BY ELIZABETH'; 124 ⟨87⟩ 'TO THE PET STORM, ON COMPLETING THE SEC- | OND YEAR OF HIS HAPPY LIFE—HOPE END, | DECEMBER 28, 1816'; 126 ⟨88⟩ 'Sweet is the perfume of apples and shaddocks,'; 128 ⟨89⟩ 'MARY MADDOX'; 129 ⟨90⟩ 'BRO', ⟨91⟩ 'BA', ⟨92⟩ 'ADDLES'; 130 ⟨93⟩ 'PAPA', ⟨94⟩ 'MARY BARRETT', ⟨95⟩ 'MUMMY'; 132 ⟨96⟩ 'BRO'S LAMENT OVER A POCKET HANDKERCHIEF'; 133 ⟨97⟩ 'TRANSLATION FROM DANTE | INFERNO, LINES 1 to 27'; 135 ⟨98⟩ 'IMPROMPTU | ON A CANDLESTICK'; 136 ⟨99⟩ 'Celestial Hope thy healing dews'; 137 ⟨100⟩ 'A VISION'; 140 ⟨101⟩ '. . . [Hea]venly bodies under the fostering sway/of a Newton!'; 141 ⟨102⟩ 'My child!! my hope and art thou dead'; 143 ⟨103⟩ 'A BIRTHDAY ODE TO HER BROTHER SAM'; 146 ⟨104⟩ 'WRITTEN IN THE ANGUISH OF BIDDING | FAREWELL TO MY BELOVED BRO—'; 148 ⟨105⟩ 'Though I am unable to swell into the sublime . . . '; 150 ⟨106⟩ '[PRINCESS CAROLINE OF BRUNSWICK AND HER | DAUGHTER]'; [163] fly title 'APPENDIX | NOTES ON A TRIP TO PARIS | OCTOBER AND NOVEMBER, 1815'; [164] blank; 165 text; [174] device of the DE VINNE PRESS; 1 blank leaf.

Vol. 2 [1] fly title 'POETRY AND PROSE FROM THE | BARRETT-BROWNING COLLECTIONS | HOPE END TO CASA GUIDI'; [2] blank; 3 text; 4 'Sketch of | My own life and reflections'; 9 'Translation from Plato . . . Diagolgue | between Criton and Socrates.'; 10 ' "Anacreon," the ladies say,'; 11 'CLEODAMUS AND MYRSON | TRANSLATED FROM THE GREEK OF BION'; 12 'TRANSLATION OF THE NINTH SATIRE | OF HORACE'S FIRST BOOK'; 21 'TRANSLATION FROM CLAU-DIAN'; 22 'TO | Thomas Campbell, Esqr.'; 24 'THE ENCHAN-TRESS'; 26 'Above th' Egean wave, the sun is glancing—'; 31 'THOUGHTS AWAKENED BY CONTEMPLATING A | PIECE OF THE PALM WHICH GROWS ON THE | SUMMIT OF THE ATHENIAN ACROPOLIS'; 34 'WRITTEN ON DEAREST STORMY'S BIRTHDAY— | HOPE END DECR 28TH 1824'; 37 ' 'neath Thy gentleness of praise,'; 38 'I sent a message to the Muse,'; 40 'RHYME AND REASON'; 43 'I could not speak the words, if words could speak/my love'; 45 'PROLOGUE'; 48 'TO MY DEAREST PAPA | ON HIS BIRTHDAY, 1825'; 50 'THE ROSE AND ZEPHYR'; 53 'IRREGULAR STANZAS'; 57 'THE BLACK STATUE'; 62 'MEDITATIONS'; 64 'REMARKS OF ELIZABETH BARRETT ON PROOF | SHEETS OF A WORK BY UVEDALE PRICE'; 71 'Who art thou of the veiled counte-nance,'; 75 ⟨text of a conversation between E.B.B. and her father concerning her composition of a poem 'On the Development of Genius'⟩; 79 'THE POETS' ENCHIRIDION'; 83 'TO UVEDALE PRICE, ESQR | ON HIS BIRTHDAY | MARCH 26, 1827'; 87 'MY BELOVED GRANNY AND TRIPPY,'; 95 'TO MY BE-LOVED MAMA, | MAY 1ST 1828'; 97 'My thoughts are far. I think upon the time,'; 99 'THE DEVELOPMENT OF GENIUS | PART I'; 114 'PART II'; 121 'PART III'; 134 'NUMBER OF LINES WHICH I CAN REPEAT | Greek Prose.'; 135 'Greek verse.'; 137 'THE REFORM BILL'; 141 '[STANZAS ADDRESSED TO HUGH STUART BOYD | WITH A TRANSLATION OF THE | "PROMETHEUS BOUND" OF ÆSCHYLUS]'; 143 'TO MARY HUNTER, ON HER BIRTHDAY, | SEPT. 11, 1833. FROM HER AFFECTIONATE E.B.B.'; 145 'THE STUDENT'; 149 'TO MARY | WRITTEN IN THE BOOK SHE MADE HERSELF, | AND GAVE ME'; 154 'STANZAS ADDRESSED TO MISS LANDON | SUGGESTED BY HER "STANZAS ON THE DEATH OF | MRS. HEMANS" '; 155 'SONG'; 157 'ORIGINAL PAPERS | [*short rule*] | A THOUGHT ON THOUGHTS'; 172 'THE HEART'; 174 'SONG'; 175 'THE MAIDEN'S DEATH'; 176 'THE PESTILENCE'; 179 'TO E.W.C. PAINTING MY PICTURE'; 180 'WISDOM UNAPPLIED'; 182 ' A SUNSET'; 185 'CATARINA TO CAMOENS'; 187 'THE STATESMAN'S FUNERAL'; 190 'CHANGES'; 191 'Fieschi's fate to French-men seems the goal of bliss/to touch!'; 192 'The moon looks downward on the earth—'; 193 'Then lightening sh[oul]d for lightening flash'; 194 'Your lyrics found me dull as prose', 'I said! when lo my birds of peace'; 195 'Have any dreamt that when the cross/In mystic darkness rested—', 'Deserted? Who hath dreamt that when'; 196 'You might be elated'; 203 [early outline of *Psyche Apocalypte*]; 205 ⟨another version of the outline⟩; 207 'PSYCHE APOCALYPTIC | A Lyrical Drama'; 222 'THREE HYMNS, | *Translated from the Greek of Gregory Nazianzen.*'; 224 '*Hymn I.*'; 225 '*Hymn II.*'; 226 '*An Evening Hymn.*'; 229 'THE MAIDEN'S DEATH: | A NEW VERSION'; 234 'TO G B H NOVEMBER 2, 1844'; 236 'THE FIRST CANTO OF DANTE'S INFERNO | DONE INTO TERZA RIMA | IN ENGLISH BY | ELIZABETH BARRETT BROWNING'; 244 device of the DE VINNE PRESS.

Plates: Vol. 1 Between leaves [1₂] and [1₃] are inserted three engraved plates. The first is a certificate of issue of the Bibliophile Society with a statement that the edition is limited to 453 copies for members only; verso blank. The second is a portrait frontispiece with tissue guard on which is printed in red 'ELIZABETH B. BARRETT.' The third is the title leaf. On the verso 'Copyright, 1914, by | THE BIBLIOPHILE SOCIETY | [*short rule*] | *All rights reserved*'. The first and third plates are mistakenly counted in the pagination as pages [iii–iv] and [v–vi] respectively. Between leaves [4₁] and [4₂] is inserted a single sheet folded once upon which is a photograph of the manuscript of 'GLIMPSES INTO MY OWN LIFE AND LITERARY CHARACTER.' Vol. 2 Between leaves [1₁] and [1₂] are inserted three engraved plates. The first is the certificate of issue as in Vol. 1; verso blank. The second is a portrait frontispiece with tissue guard on which is printed in red 'ELIZABETH BARRETT BROWNING'. The third is the title leaf, recto and verso as in Vol. 1. Both title leaves are printed from the same plate; on neither is there any indication the book is in two volumes, or which volume is number one and which is number two. Between leaves [15₂] and [15₁] is inserted a single sheet upon which is a photograph of the manuscript of 'The Maiden's Death'.

Typography and paper: Vol. 1 Unsigned. There are no running titles. Pagination centered at the bottom of the page in ornamental brackets. Text irregular, 27 lines + direction line. Leaf [15₄ʳ] type page measures 13.7 (14.5) × 9.2 cm. Gutter margins measure, pp. 56–57 = 5.0 cm; 88–89 = 5.2 cm; 136–137 = 5.0 cm. White wove paper watermarked Strathmore Japan. Sheets bulk 2.0 cm. Vol. 2 unsigned with the typographical features of Vol. 1. Gutter margins measure, pp. 88–89 = 5.1 cm; 120–121 = 5.1 cm; 152–153 = 5.1 cm. Sheets bulk 1.9 cm.

Binding: Brown leather. Sides gilt stamped at top, bottom, and fore edge with a frame of two rules. Spine: '[*two rules*] | ELIZA-BETH | BARRETT | BROWNING | [*short rule*] | VOL. I [II] | [*seal of the Bibliophile Society*] | 1914 | [*two rules*]'. All in gilt. White wove end papers. Ten stab holes at inner margin. Double binder's leaves at front and back of each volume. Top edge gilt; fore edge unopened; bottom edge trimmed. Both volumes boxed.

Notes: Some of the contents previously published in periodicals, privately printed, or published in *New Poems*, 1914. The majority of the material obtained in the Sotheby sale of 1913. In his bibliography of E.B.B. Thomas J. Wise says of this publication, "The whole are welcome, and to gather, collate, and print them was to render good service to literature. But to style the collection as it stands '*Hitherto Unpublished Poems and Stories*,' without any qualification whatever, was simply to lead astray intending subscribers to the work." The edition consisted of 453 copies and sold at $34.00.

Copies examined: TxWB TxU IU MB MWelC L.

B10 : New Poems 1914

NEW POEMS | BY | ROBERT BROWNING | AND ELIZABETH BARRETT BROWNING | EDITED BY | SIR FREDERIC G. KENYON | K.C.B., D. LITT. | *WITH TWO PORTRAITS* | LONDON | SMITH, ELDER, & CO., 15 WATERLOO PLACE | 1914

Special imprints: (p. 184 at the center) PRINTED BY | SPOTTISWOODE AND CO. LTD., COLCHESTER | LONDON AND ETON

Collation: 17.5 × 11.8 cm; [a]^8 b^8 B–M^8 N^4; 108 leaves.

Pagination: [i–v] vi–vii [viii–ix] x–xxv [xxvi–xxvii] xxviii–xxix [xxx–xxxii], [1–3] 4–73 [74–76] 77–179 [180–181] 182 [183] 184.

Contents: [i] half title 'NEW POEMS | BY | ROBERT AND MRS. BROWNING'; [ii] blank; [iii] title; [iv] blank; [v] 'PUBLISHERS' NOTE dated '*November* 1914'; [ix] 'OF THE BROWNING MSS.' signed 'FREDERIC G. KENYON.'; [xxvi] blank; [xxvii] 'CONTENTS'; [xxx] blank; [xxxi] 'PORTRAITS'; [xxxii] blank; [1] fly title 'NEW POEMS'; [2] blank; [3] 'NEW POEMS | *THE FIRST BORN OF EGYPT*'; 8 '*THE DANCE OF DEATH*'; 13 '*THE EARLIEST POEMS OF ROBERT* | *BROWNING*'; 21 '*SONNET*'; 23 '*A FOREST THOUGHT*'; 26 '*THE 'MOSES' OF MICHAEL ANGELO*'; 27 '*BEN KARSHOOK'S WISDOM*'; 29

'ON BEING DEFIED TO EXPRESS IN A HEXA– | METER: |
"YOU OUGHT TO SIT ON THE SAFETY–VALVE";' 30 'LINES
TO THE MEMORY OF HIS | PARENTS (1866)'; 31 'A ROUND
ROBIN'; 33 'HELEN'S TOWER'; 35 'OH LOVE, LOVE'; 37
'VERSES FROM 'THE HOUR WILL COME''; 39 'TRANSLA-
TION FROM PINDAR'S SEVENTH | OLYMPIAN, EPODE III.';
41 'SONNET TO RAWDON BROWN'; 43 'GOLDONI'; 45 'ON
SINGERS'; 46 'GEROUSIOS OINOS'; 49 'THE FOUNDER OF
THE FEAST | (To Arthur Chappell)'; 51 'THE NAMES'; (To
Shakespeare)'; 53 'WHY I AM A LIBERAL'; 55 'LINES FOR
THE TOMB OF LEVI LINCOLN | THAXTER'; 56 'EPPS'; 60
'THE ISLE'S ENCHANTRESS'; 61 'UNFINISHED DRAFT OF
A POEM WHICH MAY | BE ENTITLED 'ÆSCHYLUS' SOLIL-
OQUY'; 68 'JOAN OF ARC AND THE KINGFISHER'; 69 'A
SCENE IN THE BUILDING OF THE | INQUSITORS AT AN-
TWERP'; 70 'REPLY TO A TELEGRAPHIC GREETING'; 71
'REPLIES TO CHALLENGES TO RHYME'; 73 'THE DOGMA
TRIUMPHANT'; [74] blank; 75 fly title 'POEMS BY | ELIZA-
BETH BARRETT BROWNING'; [76] blank; 77 'THE EN-
CHANTRESS'; 83 'LEILA: A TALE'; 112 'A TRUE DREAM'; 119
'EPISTLE TO A CANARY'; 132 'THE MAIDEN'S DEATH'; 134
'TO ROBERT LYTTON'; 139 'MISS ELIZABETH BARRETT
BARRETT'S | CRITICISMS ON SOME OF HER FUTURE |
HUSBAND'S POEMS (1845), 'A SOUL'S TRAGEDY'; 140 'THE
FLOWER'S NAME'; 'SIBRANDUS SCHAFNBURGENSIS'; 142
'THE BOY AND THE ANGEL'; 144 'THE TOMB AT ST. PRAX-
ED'S'; 'THE LABORATORY'; 145 'ENGLAND IN ITALY. AU-
TUMN AT | SORRENTO'; 149 'ITALY IN ENGLAND'; 150
'PICTOR IGNOTUS–FLORENCE'; 151 'THE CONFESSION-
AL'; 152 'GHENT TO AIX'; 154 'TIME'S REVENGES'; 155
'SAUL'; 159 'LURIA'; 174 'ROBERT BROWNING'S ANSWERS
TO QUESTIONS | CONCERNING SOME OF HIS POEMS | By
A. Allen Brockington'; [180] blank; [181] 'INDEX TO TITLES OF
POEMS'; [183] 'INDEX TO FIRST LINES OF POEMS'; 184
printer's imprint.

Plates: Between leaves [a1] and [a2] is inserted an engraved portrait frontispiece of Robert Browning with tissue guard. Between
leaves F6 and F7 is inserted an engraved portrait of E. B. Browning with tissue guard.

Typography and paper: $1,2 (–B1, N2) signed toward outer mar-
gin of foot. Running titles set in italic rom. caps. on versos as 'NEW
POEMS' and on rectos with the title of the individual works as
'THE ENCHANTRESS'. Pagination set in the outer margin of the
headline except page numbers 13, 21, 23, 27, 29, 31, 33, 35, 37, 39,

41, 43, 45, 49, 51, 53, 55, 61, 69, 71, 73, 77, 83, 119, 139, 174 which are centered at the top. Text irregular, 26 lines + headline and direction line. Leal Fl^r type page measures 12.7 (13.8) × 8.1 cm. Gutter margins measure, pp. 56–57=3.0 cm; 88–89=3.4 cm; 120–121= 3.4 cm. White laid paper, chain lines 2.5 cm apart. Watermarked with a crown and in Gothic script '𝕬𝖇𝖇𝖊𝖞 𝕸𝖎𝖑𝖑𝖘 | 𝕲𝖗𝖊𝖊𝖓𝖋𝖎𝖊𝖑𝖉.' Sheets bulk 2.1 cm.

Binding: Olive green diagonally ribbed (S) cloth. Sides have a single vertical rule stamped in black. Spine: olive green pebble grain (P) cloth. '[*two rules*] | [*ornament*] [*three rules*] | NEW POEMS | BY | ROBERT | AND | M$^{\underline{RS}}$ BROWNING | [*three rules*] | [*ornament*] | [*three rules*] | [*ornament*] | [*three rules*] | [*ornament*] | SMITH, ELDER & C$^{\underline{o}}$ | [*two rules*]'. All rules stamped in black; all lettering and ornaments stamped in gilt. White wove end papers. Top edge trimmed; fore edge unopened; bottom edge untrimmed.

Notes: Published 28 November 1914 at five shillings. The contents chiefly derived from the Browning sale at Sothebys in 1913. The poem ascribed to E.B.B. entitled "To Robert Lytton" was not written by her, but by Lytton himself.

Copies examined: TxWB MWelC L CaOTU.

B11 : Letters to Robert Browning 1916

LETTERS | TO | ROBERT BROWNING | AND OTHER CORRESPONDENTS | BY | ELIZABETH BARRETT BROWNING | EDITED BY | THOMAS J. WISE | LONDON | PRINTED FOR PRIVATE CIRCULATION | 1916.

Special imprint: (p. [55] at the center) LONDON: | Printed for THOMAS J. WISE, Hampstead, N.W. | *Edition limited to Thirty Copies*.

Collation: 19.2 × 12.8 cm; [A]^8 B–C^8 D^4; 28 leaves.

Pagination: [1–9] 10 [11] 12–15 [16] 17–22 [23] 24–28 [29] 30–33 [34] 35–38 [39] 40–44 [45] 46–53 [54–56].

Contents: [1] half title; [2] blank; [3] blank; [4] illustration; [5] title page; [6] blank; [7] 'NOTE' signed 'T.J.W.'; [8] blank; [9] 'LETTER I. | *To* ROBERT BROWNING | [FLORENCE, 1849.]'; [11] 'LETTER II. | *To* UVEDALE PRICE, ESQ. | HOPE END, | *June*, 1826.'; [16] 'LETTER III. | *To* MISS ISA BLAGDEN. | FLORENCE, *March* 3rd, 1853'; [23] 'LETTER IV. | *To* MISS ISA

BLAGDEN. | FLORENCE, | *June 1st*, 1853.'; [29] 'LETTER V. | *To* MISS SARIANNA BROWNING. | FLORENCE, | *July 2nd*, 1857.'; [34] 'LETTER VI. | *To* MISS SARIANNA BROWNING. | (*Written by Robert Browning*) | ROME, | *Thursday, October 1st*, 1857.'; 36 '(*Written by Elizabeth Browning*)'; [39] 'LETTER VII. | *To* MISS SARIANNA BROWNING. | ROME, | *May 10th*, 1859.'; [45] 'LETTER VIII. | *To* MISS SARIANNA BROWNING. | ROME, | *February 18th*, 1860.'; [54] blank; [55] imprint; [56] blank.

Typography and paper: $1,2 signed toward outer margin of foot. Running titles set in rom. caps. as 'LETTERS TO ROBERT BROWNING'. Pagination set in the outer margin of the headline. Text 20 lines + headline and direction line. Leaf C2^r type page measures 12.1 (13.3) × 7.7 cm. All gutter margins measure 3.4 cm. White wove paper, unwatermarked. Sheets bulk 0.3 cm.

Binding: Tan paper wrappers. On front, typography identical to title page. Back wrapper blank. Six stab holes at inner margin. Top and fore edges unopened; bottom edge trimmed.

Notes: This pamphlet might better be entitled A Letter . . . rather than Letters to Robert Browning, for the only correspondence from E.B.B. to her husband here printed is an undated note of sixty-five words. As the contents reveal, all other correspondence is written to Isa Blagden and Sarianna Browning.

Copies examined: TxU MWelC L O.

B12 : Charles Dickens 1919

CHARLES DICKENS | AND | OTHER 'SPIRITS OF THE AGE' | DISCUSSED AND ANALYSED | BY | ELIZABETH BARRETT BROWNING | LONDON: | PRINTED FOR PRIVATE CIRCULATION ONLY | BY RICHARD CLAY AND SONS, LTD. | 1919.

Special imprint: (p. [19] at the center) LONDON: | Printed for THOMAS J. WISE, Hampstead, N.W. | *Edition limited to Thirty Copies*.

Collation: 19.5 × 12.8 cm; [A]^{10}; 10 leaves.

Pagination: [1–4] 5–18 [19–20].

Contents: [1] half title 'CHARLES DICKENS | AND OTHER 'SPIRITS OF THE AGE'; [2] blank; [3] title page; [4] blank; 5

'PREFACE' signed 'T.J.W.'; 7 'LETTER I' from EBB to Richard Henry Horne '*February 6th*, 1844.'; 14 'LETTER II' from EBB to Richard H. Horne '*June 9th*, 1844. | Friday night, ten o'clock.'; [19] imprint; [20] blank.

Typography and paper: Unsigned. Running titles set in rom. caps. as 'CHARLES DICKENS'. Pagination set in the outer margin of the headline except pages 5, 7, 14 which are centered at the foot of the page. Text 20 lines + headline and direction line. Leaf [A6^r] type page measures 12.0 (12.6) × 7.7 cm. The single gutter margin, pp. 10–11 measures 3.4 cm. White wove paper unwatermarked. Sheets bulk 0.1+ cm.

Binding: Brown paper wrappers. On front typography identical to title page. Back wrapper blank. Three stab holes at inner margin. Top and fore edges unopened; bottom edge trimmed.

Notes: In his preface, though not on the title page, Wise mentions that the material of this pamphlet is two letters previously printed in the Barrett-Horne correspondence edited by S. R. Townshend Mayer in 1877. That the letters were entitled 'Charles Dickens' is dishonest as well as inaccurate, for the purpose of the first letter is to ask Horne not to send any more proofs of his *A New Spirit of the Age* to E.B.B. while he is out of town, and the second concerns Horne's sensitivity to the criticism of his contemporaries. For the record the word 'Dickens' appears only once in the entire pamphlet, and no more than 5 lines in a total of 130 in the first letter, and 9 lines in a total of 70 in the second letter refer to him. Some curious variants occur in the comparison of Mayer's transcriptions of the letters and those of Wise here. For example in the first paragraph of Letter I the former version reads, "Therefore no proofs while you are out of town—unless, as I said, I can do any good in correcting". But the latter version reads, "Therefore no proofs while you are out of town—unless as I said, I can do any good in proportion to the risk of evil."

Copies examined: TxU TxWB MWelC L O.

B13 : Edgar Allan Poe 1919

EDGAR ALLAN POE | A CRITICISM | WITH REMARKS ON THE MORALS AND RELIGION | OF | SHELLY AND LEIGH HUNT | BY | ELIZABETH BARRETT BROWNING | LONDON: | PRINTED FOR PRIVATE CIRCULATION ONLY | BY RICHARD CLAY AND SONS, LTD. | 1919

Special imprint: (p. [xvi] at the center) London: | Printed for
THOMAS J. WISE, Hampstead, N.W. | *Edition limited to Thirty
Copies.*

Collation: 19.3 × 12.8 cm; [A]⁸; 8 leaves.

Pagination: [1–5] 6–8 [9] 10–15 [16].

Contents: [1] half title 'EDGAR ALLAN POE | A CRITICISM';
[2] blank; [3] title page; [4] blank; [5] 'LETTER I' from E.B.B.
to Richard Henry Horne, '50, Wimpole Street, | London. | *May
12th,* 1845.'; [9] 'LETTER II' from EBB to Richard Henry Horne
'*December,* 1843. | *Wednesday*'; [16] imprint.

Typography and paper: Unsigned. Running titles set in rom. caps.
as 'EDGAR ALLAN POE'. Pagination set in the outer margin of
the headline. Text, 20 lines + headline. Leaf [A6ʳ] type page
measures 12.1 (12.7) × 7.8 cm. The single gutter margin, pp.
8–[9] measures 3.4 cm. White wove paper unwatermarked. Sheets
bulk 0.1 + cm.

Binding: Orange coated paper wrappers. On front typography
identical to title page. Back wrapper blank. Three stab holes at
inner margin. Top and fore edges unopened, bottom edge untrimmed.

Notes: Although Wise had received permission from Smith, Elder,
and Co., the holders of Browning Copyright in 1919, to publish the
letters written by E.B.B., his selection of the title used flagrantly
deceived both scholars and collectors concerning the nature of the
pamphlet's contents. Nowhere on the wrapper or title page is there
any indication that the material printed was letters, not intended
for publication, rather than essays of literary criticism. Further-
more, the purpose of the first letter was E.B.B.'s thanking Horne
for the gift of a book, and the second was to accompany the return
of the proofs of Horne's *A New Spirit of the Age*. Nothing what-
soever is said by E.B.B. about Leigh Hunt's morals, what is quoted
is a statement allegedly made about Hunt by Mary Russell Mitford. Her remarks about Edgar Allan Poe are in reference to the
reviews he published of E.B.B.'s works in America, and were in no
way written as criticism. I have not seen the originals of these
letters, but it was not above Wise to rearrange the paragraph
structure, italicize phrases not underlined, and to omit material
without notice of ellipisis. Until the letters can be collated, caution
should be exercised in drawing conclusions from their contents.

Copies examined: TxU TxWB IaU MWelC L O.

B14 : Alfred Tennyson 1919

ALFRED TENNYSON | NOTES AND COMMENTS | WITH |
A DEFENCE OF THE RHYME SYSTEM OF | "THE DEAD
PAN" | BY | ELIZABETH BARRETT BROWNING | LONDON:
| PRINTED FOR PRIVATE CIRCULATION ONLY | BY
RICHARD CLAY AND SONS, LTD. | 1919.

Special imprint: (p. [20] at the center) LONDON; | Printed for
THOMAS J. WISE, Hampstead, N.W. | *Edition limited to Thirty
Copies.*

Collation: 19.2 × 12.7 cm; [A]¹⁰; 10 leaves.

Pagination: [1–4] 5–19 [20].

Contents: [1] half title 'ALFRED TENNYSON'; [2] blank; [3]
title page; [4] blank; 5 'LETTER I' from E.B.B. to Richard Henry
Horne '50, Wimpole Street, | London. | *December* 16th, 1843.'; 11
'LETTER II' from E.B.B. to Richard Henry Horne '[50, Wimpole
Street, | London.] | Thursday. | [Post mark *July* 20th, 1844]'; [20]
imprint.

Typography and paper: Unsigned. Running titles set in rom. caps.
as 'ALFRED TENNYSON'. Pagination set in outer margin of the
headline except pages 5 and 11 which are centered at the foot of
the page. Text 20 lines + headline and direction line. Leaf [A7ʳ]
type page measures 12.0 (12.6) × 7.8 cm. The single gutter
margin, pp. 10–11 measures 3.4 cm. White wove paper unwatermarked. Sheets bulk 0.1+ cm.

Binding: Blue paper wrappers. On front typography identical to
title page. Back wrapper blank. Three stab holes at inner margin.
Top and fore edges unopened; bottom edges untrimmed.

Notes: In letter I, Tennyson is mentioned in passing with other
comments about Harriet Martineau, Lough's bust of Southy, and
a particular issue of *Blackwood's*, not specified. Letter II is a reply
to Horne's criticism of E.B.B.'s manuscript 'The Dead Pan' which
was about to be published in her *Poems*, 1844. Neither letter, of
course, was written as a formal prose essay.

Copies examined: TxU MWelC L O ICU.

B15 : William Wordsworth 1919

A NOTE ON | WILLIAM WORDSWORTH | WITH A STATE-
MENT OF HER VIEWS | ON SPIRITUALISM | BY | ELIZA-

BETH BARRETT BROWNING | LONDON: | PRINTED FOR
PRIVATE CIRCULATION ONLY | BY RICHARD CLAY AND
SONS, LTD. | 1919.

Special imprint: (p. [19] at the center) LONDON: | Printed for
THOMAS J. WISE, Hampstead, N.W. | *Edition limited to Thirty
Copies.*

Collation: 19.2 × 12.7; [A]¹⁰; 10 leaves.

Pagination: [1–5] 6–7 [8] 9–17 [18–20].

Contents: [1] half title 'A NOTE ON | WILLIAM WORDS-
WORTH'; [2] blank; [3] title page; [4] blank; [5] 'LETTER I'
from E.B.B. to Richard Henry Horne '50, Wimpole St. | LONDON.
| [*Circa* 1843.]'; [8] 'LETTER II' from E.B.B. to Mary Hunter '28,
VIA DEL FRITONE, | ROME. | *December* 31*st*. [1859]; [18]
blank; [19] imprint; [20] blank.

Typography and paper: Unsigned. Running titles set in rom. caps.
on versos as 'A NOTE ON' and on rectos as 'WILLIAM WORDS-
WORTH'. Pagination set in the outer margin of the headline. Text
20 lines + headline. Leaf [A6ʳ] type page measures 12.0 (12.6+)
× 7.7 cm. The single gutter margin, pp. 10–11 measures 3.4 cm.
White wove paper unwatermarked. Sheets bulk 0.1 + cm. In some
copies the comma after the word WISE in the printer's imprint is
heavily battered.

Binding: Pink paper wrappers. On front typography identical to
title page. Back wrapper blank. Three stab holes at inner margin.
Top and fore edges unopened; bottom edge untrimmed.

Notes: Letter I here simply contains E.B.B.'s reactions to Horne's
comments about Wordsworth, after she had read the proofs for
his book, A *New Spirit of the Age.* Mayer's transcription of this
same letter lacks a paragraph and has textual variants not found
in the version by Wise. Letter II from E.B.B. to Mary Hunter
mainly discusses her life in Italy, and is hardly a definitive 'Statement' by the poet about spiritualism as suggested by the title.

Copies examined: TxU TxWB MWelC L O.

The Barlow engraving after a photograph by Macaire; first printed as the frontispiece for her *Letters to R. H. Horne.*

Savage tongues, that wont to fling

Savage tongues ,that wont to fling

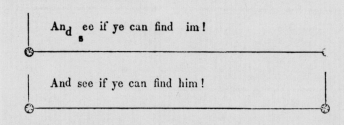

And$_d$ ee if ye can find im !

And see if ye can find him !

'You're slow in sending home the work,—I count
'I've waited near an hour for't.' Pardon me,—

'You' re slow in sending home the work,—I coun^t
'I've waited near an hour for't.' Pardon me,—

This was different: scarce as loud perhaps, (who

This was different: scarce as loud perhaps, (who

States and concealed impressions discovered by Hinman Collation, entries A3, A5a, A11, and A12.

A Curse for a Nation
By Elizabeth Barrett Browning.

Prologue.

I heard an angel speak last night
        And he said, "Write!
Write a nation's curse for me
And send it over the western sea.

I faltered, taking up the word.
        "Not so, my Lord!
If curses must be, ~~choose~~ another
To send thy curse against my brother.

For I am bound by ~~love or blood~~ gratitude
        ~~My love & blood~~ And gratitude
To brothers of mine across the sea
Who have stretched out kindly hands to me.

Therefore, the voice said, shall thou write
        "My curse tonight:
From the summits of love a curse is driven
As lightning ~~is~~ from the tops of heaven.

Not so, I answered; evermore
        My heart is sore
For my own land's sins: for the little feet
Of children bleeding along the street.

For parked=up honours that gainsay
        The right of way;
For almsgiving through a door that is
Not open enough for two friends to kiss.

Manuscript page, heavily revised of "A Curse for a Nation," Miriam
Lutcher Stark Library, The University of Texas.

T W O   P O E M S

BY

ELIZABETH BARRETT AND ROBERT
BROWNING.

LONDON:

CHAPMAN & HALL, 193, PICCADILLY.

1854.

Front wrapper of E.B.B.'s and R.B.'s *Two Poems*. This may have suggested the format for Thomas J. Wise's forgery, *The Runaway Slave at Pilgrim's Point*, reproduced on the following leaf.

THE

RUNAWAY SLAVE

AT PILGRIM'S POINT.

BY

ELIZABETH BARRETT BROWNING.

LONDON:

CHAPMAN & HALL, 193 PICCADILLY.

1849.

Front wrapper of *The Runaway Slave at Pilgrim's Point*. First impression. Two copies only are extant. University of Texas copy.

AURORA LEIGH.

BY

ELIZABETH BARRETT BROWNING.

THIRD EDITION.

LONDON:
CHAPMAN AND HALL, 193, PICCADILLY.
1857.

Title page of *Aurora Leigh*. Third edition. This has been perennially reported as a ghost. Leeds University Copy.

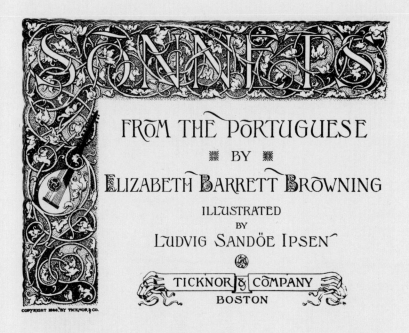

SONNETS

FROM THE PORTUGUESE

❋ BY ❋

ELIZABETH BARRETT BROWNING

ILLUSTRATED
BY
LUDVIG SANDÖE IPSEN

TICKNOR & COMPANY
BOSTON

Title page of *Sonnets from the Portuguese*, published by Tickner & Co.,
Boston in 1886. This was the genuine first published edition of the work.

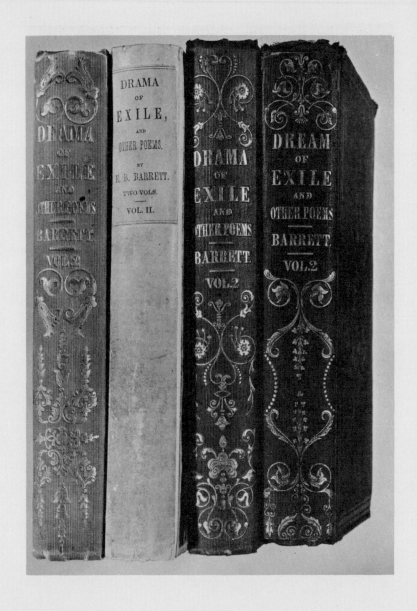

Binding variants of *A Drama of Exile*. Yale University copies.

CONTRIBUTIONS

C : CONTRIBUTIONS TO PERIODICALS,
NEWSPAPERS, GIFTS BOOKS AND
ANTHOLOGIES

C1 : Stanzas, Excited by Some Reflections on the Present State of Greece, *New Monthly Magazine*, Second Series, I (1821), 523.

C2 : Thoughts Awakened by Contemplating a Piece of the Palm Which Grows on the Summit of the Acropolis at Athens, *New Monthly Magazine*, Second Series, II (1821), 59.

C3 : Stanzas on the Death of Lord Byron, London *Globe and Traveller*, 30 June 1824.

C4 : The Rose and Zephyr, *Literary Gazette, and Journal of the Belles Lettres* (19 November 1825), 750.

C5 : Irregular Stanzas, *Literary Gazette, and Journal of the Belles Lettres* (6 May 1826), 284.

C6 : [Who art thou of the veiléd countenance,] *Jewish Expositor, and Friend of Israel*, XII (January 1827), 14–16.

C7 : Kings, *The Times*, 31 May 1831.

C8 : The Pestilence, *The Times*, 13 January 1832.

C9 : Stanzas Addressed to Miss Landon, and Suggested by Her 'Stanzas on the Death of Mrs. Hemans,' *New Monthly Magazine*, XLV (September 1835), 82.

C10 : Man and Nature, *Athenaeum* (19 March 1836), 208.

C11 : The Seaside Walk, *Athenaeum* (2 July 1836), 468.

C12 : The Romaunt of Margret, *New Monthly Magazine*, XLVII (July 1836), 316–320.

C13 : A Thought on Thoughts, *Athenaeum* (23 July 1836), 522–523.

C14 : The Poet's Vow, *New Monthly Magazine*, XLVIII (October 1836), 209–218.

C15 : The Island, *New Monthly Magazine*, XLIX (January 1837), 22–25.

C16 : The Young Queen, *Athenaeum* (1 July 1837), 483.

C17 : Victoria's Tears, *Athenaeum*, (8 July 1837), 506.

C18 : A Romance of the Ganges, *Findens' Tableaux: a Series of Picturesque Scenes of National Character, Beauty, and Costume*, ed. Mary Russell Mitford (London 1838), 29–31.

C19 : The Romaunt of the Page, *Findens' Tableaux of the Affections: A Series of Picturesque Illustrations of the Womanly Virtues*, ed. Mary Russell Mitford (London 1839), 1–5.

c20 : A Sabbath on the Sea, *The Amaranth: A Miscellany of Original Prose and Verse*, ed. T. K. Hervey (London 1839), 73–75.

c21 : L.E.L.'s Last Question, *Athenaeum* (26 January 1839), 69.

c22 : The Crowned and Wedded Queen, *Athenaeum* (15 February 1840), 131.

c23 : The Dream, *Findens' Tableaux: the Iris of Prose, Poetry, and Art for 1840*, ed. Mary Russell Mitford (London 1840), 7–8.

c24 : The Legend of the Brown Rosarie, the same, 15–21.

c25 : A Night Watch by the Sea, *Monthly Chronicle*, V (April 1840), 297.

c26 : A Lay of the Rose, *Monthly Chronicle*, VI (July 1840), 13–17.

c27 : Napoleon's Return, *Athenaeum* (4 July 1840), 532.

c28 : The House of Clouds, *Athenaeum* (21 August 1841), 643.

c29 : Lessons from the Gorse, *Athenaeum* (23 October 1841), 810.

c30 : Queen Annelida and False Arcite, *The Poems of Geoffrey Chaucer Modernized*, ed. R. H. Horne (London 1841), 237–247.

c31 : The Complaint of Annelida to False Arcite, the same, 248.

c32 : Three Hymns, Translated from the Greek of Gregory Nazianzen, *Athenaeum*, (8 January 1842), 39–40.

c33 : Some Account of the Greek Christian Poets, *Athenaeum* (26 February 1842), 189–90; (5 March 1842), 210–212; (12 March 1842), 229–231; (19 March 1842), 249–252.

c34 : The Book of the Poets, *Athenaeum* (4 June 1842), 497–499; (11 June 1842), 520–523; (25 June 1842), 558–560; (6 August 1842), 706–708; (13 August 1842), 728–729.

c35 : *Poems, Chiefly of Early and Late Years, including the Borderers, a Tragedy*. By William Wordsworth ⟨A review by E.B.B.⟩ *Athenaeum* (27 August 1842), 757–759.

c36 : A Claim in an Allegory, *Athenaeum* (17 September 1842), 818.

c37 : Sonnet on Mr. Haydon's Portrait of Mr. Wordsworth, *Athenaeum* (29 October 1842), 932.

c38 : The Cry of the Human, *Boston Miscellany of Literature and Fashion*, II (November 1842), 197–199.

c39 : [I tell you, hopeless grief is passionless;], *Graham's Magazine*, XXI (December 1842), 303.

c40 : [When some beloved voice, which was to you], the same, 303.

c41 : [What are we set on earth for? Say to toil!], the same, 303.

c42 : [The woman singeth at her spinning-wheel], the same, 303.

c43 : Introductory Stanzas, *Schloss's English Bijou Almanack for 1843*, Poetically Illustrated by Mary Russell Mitford. (London 1842).

c44 : The Prince of Wales, the same.

c45 : Duchess of Orleans, the same.

c46 : Rogers, the same.

c47 : The King of Prussia, the same.

c48 : The Maiden's Death, *Pioneer*, I (March 1843), 112.

c49 : Orion: an Epic Poem by R. H. Horne. ⟨a review by E.B.B.⟩ *Athenaeum* (24 June 1843), 583–584.

c50 : The Soul's Expression, *Graham's Magazine*, XXIII (July 1843), 34.

c51 : To Flush, My Dog, *Athenaeum* (22 July 1843), 670–671.

c52 : Seraph and Poet, *Graham's Magazine*, XXIII (August 1843), 71.

c53 : The Cry of the Children, *Blackwood's Edinburgh Magazine*, XLIV (August 1843), 260–262.

c54 : The Child and the Watcher, *Graham's Magazine*, XXIV (September 1843), 158.

c55 : Catarina to Camoens, *Graham's Magazine*, XXIV (October 1843), 208–209.

c56 : The Lady's Yes. A Song, *Graham's Magazine*, XXV (January 1844), 18.

c57 : Loved Once, *Graham's Magazine*, XXV (March 1844), 65.

c58 : Pain in Pleasure, *Graham's Magazine*, XXVI (August 1844), 65.

c59 : Insufficiency, *United States Magazine and Democratic Review*, New Series, XV (August 1844), 194.

c60 : Sonnet: A Sketch, *Christian Mother's Magazine*, II (October, 1845), 635.

c61 : Wisdom Unapplied, the same, 645.

c62 : A Woman's Shortcomings, *Blackwood's Edinburgh Magazine*, LX (October 1846), 488–489.

c63 : A Man's Requirements, the same, 489–490.

c64 : Maud's Spinning, the same, 490–491.

c65 : A Dead Rose, the same, 491–492.

c66 : Change on Change, the same, 492.

c67 : A Reed, the same, 492–493.

c68 : Hector in the Garden, the same, 493–495.

c69 : ⟨translation from the Odyssey of⟩ **The Daughters of Pandarus**, *Memoirs and Essays Illustrative of Art, Literature, and Social Morals*, ed. Anna Jameson (London 1846), 137–138.

c70 : Life, *Blackwood's Edinburgh Magazine*, LXI (May 1847), 555.

c71 : Love, the same, 555–556.

c72 : Heaven and Earth. 1845, the same, 556.

c73 : The Prospect. 1845, the same, 556.

c74 : Two Sketches, *Blackwood's Edinburgh Magazine*, LXI (June 1847), 683–684.

c75 : Mountaineer and Poet, the same, 684.

c76 : The Poet, the same, 684.

c77 : The Runaway Slave at Pilgrim's Point, *Liberty Bell* (Boston 1848), 29–44.

c78 : A Child's Grave at Florence, *Athenaeum* (22 December 1849), 1804.

c79 : My Kate, *Keepsake*, ed. Marguerite A. Power (London 1855), 16–17.

c80 : A Curse for a Nation, *Liberty Bell* (Boston, 1856), 1–9.

c81 : Amy's Cruelty, *Keepsake*, ed. Marguerite A. Power (London 1857), 75–76.

c82 : A Tale of Villafranca, *Athenaeum* (24 September 1859), 397–398.

c83 : A Court Lady, *Independent,* IX (29 March 1860), 1.

c84 : First News from Villafranca, *Independent,* X (7 June 1860), 1.

c85 : A Musical Instrument, *Cornhill Magazine,* II (July 1860), 84–85.

c86 : King Victor Emanuel Entering Florence, *Independent,* XII (16 August 1860), 1.

c87 : The Sword of Castruccio Castracani, *Independent,* XII (30 August 1860), 1.

c88 : Summing Up in Italy, *Independent,* XII (27 September 1860), 1.

c89 : A Forced Recruit at Soloferino, *Cornhill Magazine,* II (October 1860), 419–420.

c90 : Garibaldi, *Independent,* XII (11 October 1860), 1.

c91 : De Profundis, *Independent,* XII (6 December 1860), 1.

c92 : Parting Lovers, *Independent,* XIII (21 March 1861), 1.

c93 : Mother and Poet, *Independent,* XIII (2 May 1861), 1.

c94 : Only a Curl, *Independent,* XIII (16 May 1861), 1.

c95 : Little Mattie, *Cornhill Magazine,* III (June 1861), 736–737.

c96 : The King's Gift, *Independent,* XIII (18 July 1861), 1.

c97 : A View Across the Roman Campagna, *Independent,* XIII (25 July 1861), 1.

c98 : Psyche Apocalpyte, *St. James Magazine and United Empire Review,* ed. S. R. Townshend Mayer, II (February 1876), 478–492.

c99 : Extracts from Elizabeth Barrett's Criticisms of Some of her Future Husband's Poems, *Cornhill Magazine* (August 1913), 166–174.

c 100 : The Maiden's Death, *Cornhill Magazine* (December 1913), 721–722.

c101 : Stanzas—A Fragment, *A Bibliography of the Writings in Prose and Verse of Elizabeth Barrett Browning,* comp. T. J. Wise (London 1918), 217.

c102 : The Poet's Record, *Anthony Munday and Other Essays,* ed. E. Conway (New York 1927).

C103 : ⟨an early draft of⟩ The Cry of the Children, *Notes and Queries* (24 December 1949), 564–566.

C104 : The Poet's Enchiridion, *Studies in English*, ed. Hazel Harrod XXVII (1948), 169–177.

C105 : The Sorrows of the Muses, *Books at Iowa* 4 (1966), 19–36.

LETTERS

D

D1 : Powell, Thomas. *The Living Authors of England*. (New York, 1849), 146–152.

D2 : ⟨A letter to the editors of the *Independent*⟩, *Independent* XIII (21 March 1861), 1.

D3 : ⟨A letter to one of the editors of the *Independent*⟩, *Independent* XIII (2 May 1861), 1.

D4 : ⟨A letter to R. H. Horne⟩, *Macmillan's Magazine*, XXII (September 1870), 363–365.

D5 : Letters from Elizabeth Barrett Browning to the Author of 'Orion' on Literary and General Topics, *Contemporary Review*, XXIII (December 1873), 146–161; (January 1874), 281–302; (February 1874), 447–461; (April 1874) 799–813.

D6 : Elizabeth Barrett Browning on Some of her Contemporaries. (With Original Letters), *St. James Magazine and United Empire Review*, New Series XVII (October 1876), 21–31.

D7 : Letters to Richard H. Horne 1877.

LETTERS | OF | ELIZABETH BARRETT BROWNING | ADDRESSED TO | RICHARD HENGIST HORNE, | AUTHOR OF "ORION," "GREGORY VII.," "COSMO DE' MEDICI," ETC. | 𝔚𝔦𝔱𝔥 𝔠𝔬𝔪𝔪𝔢𝔫𝔱𝔰 𝔬𝔫 ℭ𝔬𝔫𝔱𝔢𝔪𝔭𝔬𝔯𝔞𝔯𝔦𝔢𝔰. | EDITED BY | S. R. TOWNSHEND MAYER. | VOL. I. [II.] | [*publisher's device*] | LONDON: | RICHARD BENTLEY AND SON, | 𝔓𝔲𝔟𝔩𝔦𝔰𝔥𝔢𝔯𝔰 𝔦𝔫 ℭ𝔯𝔡𝔦𝔫𝔞𝔯𝔶 𝔱𝔬 ℌ𝔢𝔯 𝔐𝔞𝔧𝔢𝔰𝔱𝔶 𝔱𝔥𝔢 ℭ𝔲𝔢𝔢𝔫, | [*short rule 0.6 cm*] | 1877.

Collation: Vol. 1 20.1 × 13.2 cm; π^6 ($-\pi$1) 1–17^8; 141 leaves. Vol. 2 20.1 × 13.2 cm; π^2 ($-\pi$1) $^2\pi^2$ 1–18^8 1–19^4; 151 leaves.

Pagination: Vol. 1 [i–v] vi–viii [ix–x], [1–3] 4–92 [93–95] 96–127 [128–131] 132–272. Vol. 2 [i–vi], [1–3] 4–57 [58–61] 62–110 [111–113] 114–195 [196–199] 200–296.

Binding: Purple diagonally ribbed (S) cloth. Front stamped in black with an ornate frame of five rules with corner points enclosing a gilt stamped arabesque. Back stamped in blind with a frame of two rules. Spine: '[*dot and line rule*] | [*dot and line rule*] | within an elaborate gilt stamped frame: LETTERS | OF | ELIZABETH | BARRETT | BROWNING | [*within a gilt frame*] HORNE | VOL. I. [II.] | [*within a frame of dots and lines*] BENTLEY' Brown coated end papers. Six stab holes at inner margin. Top and fore edges unopened; bottom edge untrimmed.

D8 : Kind Words from a Sick Room 1891.

KIND WORDS FROM A SICK ROOM. | [*double rule 2.5 cm.*] |
ELIZABETH BARRETT BARRETT | (MRS. BROWNING). |
PRIVATELY PRINTED | (BY WILLIAM HUTCHISON:
GREENOCK) | MDCCCXCI.

Collation: 22.3 × 13.7 cm; [A]⁶; 6 leaves.

Pagination: [1–3] 4–10 [2].

Binding: Gray paper wrappers; front and back blank. Top and
fore edges unopened, bottom edge untrimmed.

Note: This pamphlet contains four letters from E.B.B. to Allan
Park Paton, 1845–1846 and one letter from R. B. to Allan Park
Paton, 1883.

D9 : *The Collector: an Historical Magazine for Autograph Collectors*, V (November 1891), 34–36; (December 1891), 51–53; (January 1892) 74–76; (February 1892) 89–90; (March 1892), 105–
107.

D10 : **An Opinion on Tennyson,** *Literary Anecdotes of the Nineteenth Century*, ed. W. Robertson Nicoll and T. J. Wise (London
1895), 33–41.

Note: Not an essay as the editors suggest, but another letter from
E.B.B. to R. H. Horne concerning the material in *A New Spirit
of the Age*.

D11 : **Carlyle, A Disentangled Essay,** *Literary Anecdotes of the
Nineteenth Century*, ed. W. Robertson Nicoll and T. J. Wise (London 1896), 103–119.

Note: Part of another letter from E.B.B. to R. H. Horne.

D12 : **The Religious Opinions of Elizabeth Barrett Browning,** the
same, 121–142. See also B3.

D13 : Letters of E.B.B. ed. F. G. Kenyon 1897.

THE LETTERS | OF | ELIZABETH BARRETT BROWNING |
EDITED WITH BIOGRAPHICAL ADDITIONS | BY | FRED-
ERIC G. KENYON | *WITH PORTRAITS* | IN TWO VOLUMES |
VOLUME I. [II.] | LONDON | SMITH, ELDER, & CO., 15
WATERLOO PLACE | 1897 | [All rights reserved]

Collation: Vol. 1   19.1 × 12.2 cm; [A]⁸ B–HH⁸; 248 leaves. Vol. 2
19.1 × 12.2 cm; [A]⁴ B–GG⁸ HH⁴; 240 leaves.

Pagination: Vol. 1 [2] [i–v] vi–xi [xii–xiii] xiv, [1] 2–478 [479–480]. Vol. 2 [2] [i–v] vi, [1] 2–453 [454–455] 456–464 [465–472].

Binding: Green calico (V) cloth. Sides blind stamped with a single ruled frame. Spine: 'THE | LETTERS | OF | ELIZA-BETH | BARRETT | BROWNING | VOL. I. [II.] | SMITH, EL-DER & CO.' Black coated end papers. Eight stab holes at inner margin. Top and fore edges unopened; bottom edge untrimmed.

D14 : Letters of R.B. and E.B.B. 1845–1846 1899

THE LETTERS | OF | ROBERT BROWNING | AND | ELIZA-BETH BARRETT BARRETT | 1845–1846 | *WITH PORTRAITS AND FACSIMILES* | IN TWO VOLUMES | VOL. I. [II.] | LON-DON | SMITH, ELDER, & CO., 15 WATERLOO PLACE | 1899 | [All rights reserved]

Collation: Vol. 1 19.0 × 12.7 cm; [A]⁴ B–OO⁸ PP⁴; 292 leaves. Vol. 2 19.0 × 12.7 cm; [A]⁴ B–OO⁸ PP⁴; 292 leaves.

Pagination: Vol. I [8] [1] 2–579 [580–584]. Vol. 2 [8] [1] 2–567 [568–569] 570–579 [580–584].

Binding: Dark green calico (V) cloth. Sides blind stamped with a single rule. Spine: '[rule] | THE | LETTERS | OF | ROBERT | BROWNING | AND | ELIZABETH BARRETT | 1845–1846 | VOL. I. [II.] | SMITH, ELDER, & Cº | [rule]' All in gilt. Gray coated end papers. Eight stab holes at inner margin. Top and fore edges unopened; bottom edged untrimmed.

D15 : The Art of Scansion 1916

[*within a ruled frame 17.7 × 12.7 cm*] THE ART | OF | SCAN-SION | BY | Elizabeth Barrett Browning | WITH AN INTRO-DUCTION | BY | ALICE MEYNELL | LONDON | Privately printed by Clement Shorter, December 1916.

Collation: 26.8 × 20.9 cm; [A]¹⁶; 16 leaves.

Pagination: [4] [i–v] v [vi] vii–ix [x], 1–11 [12–14] [4].

Binding: Green paper wrappers. On front typography identical to title page. Back wrapper blank. First and last leaves used as pastedowns. Three stab holes at inner margin. Top and fore edges unopened; bottom edge untrimmed.

Notes: The text of this pamphlet is a letter from E.B.B. to Uvcdalc Price dated April 1827. Twenty-five copies only were privately printed by Clement Shorter in December, 1916.

Copies Held: TxU, L.

D16 : Letters to Robert Browning and Other Correspondents. (London, 1916). See B11.

D17 : Charles Dickens and Other 'Spirits of the Age.' (London, 1919). See B12.

D18 : Edgar Allan Poe A Criticism With Remarks on the Morals and Religion of Shelley and Leigh Hunt. (London, 1919). See B13.

D19 : Alfred Tennyson Notes and Comments With a Defence of the Rhyme System of the Dead Pan. (London, 1919). See B14.

D20 : A Note on William Wordsworth With a Statement of her View on Spiritualism. (London, 1919). See B15.

D21 : Letters to Her Sister 1929

ELIZABETH BARRETT | BROWNING: | LETTERS TO HER SISTER, 1846–1859 | EDITED BY LEONARD HUXLEY, LL.D. | WITH PORTRAITS | LONDON | JOHN MURRAY, ALBEMARLE STREET, W.

Collation: 21.8 × 13.7 cm; [A]^8 B–Y^8 Z^{10}; 186 leaves.

Pagination: [i–v] vi–viii [ix–x] xi–xxiii [xxiv] xxv [xxvi], 1–323 [324] 325–344 [345–346].

Binding: Green calico (V) cloth. Front blind stamped with a single ruled frame enclosing an ornately decorated monogram in gilt. Back blank. Spine: '[*rule*] | ELIZABETH | BARRETT | BROWNING | Letters to her | Sister | 1846–1859 | [*short rule*] | Leonard | Huxley | JOHN MURRAY | [*rule*].' All in gilt. White end papers. Ten stab holes at inner margin. All edges trimmed.

D22 : Twenty-two Unpublished Letters 1935

TWENTY-TWO | UNPUBLISHED LETTERS OF | ELIZABETH BARRETT BROWNING | AND ROBERT BROWNING | ADDRESSED TO HENRIETTA AND ARABELLA MOULTON — | BARRETT | *New York: The United Feature Syndicate* | Mcmxxxv

Collation: 24.2 × 15.7 cm; [Unsigned 1–14^4]; 56 leaves.

Pagination: [2] [i–vii] viii–x [xi–xiv], 1–89 [90–92] [4].

Binding: Gray paper covered boards; white velum backstrip. No stamping on sides. Spine: 'TWENTY | TWO | BROWNING |

LETTERS | [*ornament*] | *E. B. B.* | *and R. B.* | *to Henrietta* | *and
Arabel* | *1935'* All in gilt.

D23 : A Selection of the Barrett-Browning Correspondence 1936

FROM | ROBERT & ELIZABETH | BROWNING | *A FURTHER
SELECTION OF THE BARRETT-BROWNING FAMILY COR-
RESPONDENCE* | INTRODUCTION AND NOTES BY WIL-
LIAM ROSE BENÉT | LONDON | JOHN MURRAY, ALBE-
MARLE STREET, W.

Collation: 18.7 × 12.2 cm; [A]^8 B–I^8 K^4; 76 leaves.

Pagination: [i–vi], 1–144 [145–146].

Binding: Blue-green calico (V) cloth. On front in the upper left
hand corner are gilt stamped facsimile signatures 'Robert Browning.' and 'Elizabeth Barrett Browning.' Back blank. Spine: 'FROM
| ROBERT | AND | ELIZABETH | BROWNING | [*french rule*] |
[*french rule*] | J. M.' All in gilt. Cream end papers. Eight stab
holes at inner margin. Top edge stained blue. Fore and bottom
edges trimmed.

D24 : Letters to B. R. Haydon 1939

LETTERS | FROM ELIZABETH BARRETT | TO B. R. HAY-
DON | Edited by | MARTHA HALE SHACKFORD | Professor
of English Literature | Wellesley College | OXFORD UNIVER-
SITY PRESS | New York London Toronto | 1939.

Collation: 21.7 × 13.8 cm; [Unsigned 1–10^8]; 80 leaves.

Pagination: [2] [i–v] vi–ix [x–xiii] xiv–xlv [xlvi–xlvii] xlviii–lxx
[lxxi] lxxii, [1–3] 4–76 [77] 78 [8].

Binding: Blue calico (V) cloth. No stamping on sides. Spine:
'[*ornament*] | Letters | from | Elizabeth | Barrett | to | B. R. | Hay-
don | [*ornament*] | OXFORD' All in gilt. White wove end papers.
Ten stab holes at inner margin. Top edges stained blue; fore and
bottom edges trimmed.

D25 : An Unpublished letter of E.B.B. ⟨to Miss Elliot⟩, *Notes and
Queries* (28 October 1939), 310–311.

**D26 : Margaret Fuller and Elizabeth Barrett Browning ⟨an un-
published letter⟩**, *Notes and Queries* (24 April 1943), 252–253.

D27 : Mrs. Browning on Marriage, *Notes and Queries* (17 July
1943), 45.

D28 : A Letter by E.B.B. ⟨to Isa Blagden⟩, *More Books,* XXI (May 1946), 178–180.

D29 : Correspondence of Harriet Beecher Stowe and Elizabeth Barrett Browning, ed. Hazel Harrod, *Studies in English,* XXVII (June 1948), 28–34.

D30 : Twenty Unpublished Letters of Elizabeth Barrett to Hugh Stuart Boyd, ed. Bennett Weaver, *PMLA,* LXV (June 1950), 397–418.

D31 : An Unpublished Letter of E.B.B. ⟨to Euphrasia Fanny Haworth⟩, *Research Studies of the State College of Washington,* XVIII (September 1950), 223–224.

D32 : New Letters from Mrs. Browning to Isa Blagden, ed. Edward C. McAleer, *PMLA,* LXVI (September 1951), 594–612.

D33 : Unpublished Letters of Thomas De Quincy and Elizabeth Barrett Browning, Edited from Originals in the Grey Collection, Auckland Public Library, ed. S. Musgrove, *Auckland University College Bulletin,* No. 44. English Series No. 7, 1954.

D34 : Letters to Mary Russell Mitford 1954

ELIZABETH BARRETT | to | MISS MITFORD | [*french rule 5.9 cm.*] | THE UNPUBLISHED LETTERS OF | ELIZABETH BARRETT BARRETT | TO MARY RUSSELL MITFORD | EDITED AND INTRODUCED BY | BETTY MILLER | [*star*] | LONDON | JOHN MURRAY, ALBEMARLE ST | 1954

Collation: 21.5 × 13.8 cm; [A]¹⁰ B–S⁸ T⁶; 152 leaves

Pagination: [i–iv] v–xviii [xix–xx]; 1–275 [276] 277–284.

Binding: Venetian red linen. On the front in the upper left corner are gilt stamped facsimile signatures 'M. R. Mitford' and 'Elizabeth Barrett Barrett.' No stamping on back. Spine: 'ELIZABETH BARRETT | to | MISS MITFORD | [*star*] | BETTY | MILLER | [*star*] | JOHN MURRAY' All in gilt. White wove end papers. Ten stab holes at inner margin. All edges trimmed.

D35 : Letters to Hugh Stuart Boyd 1955

Elizabeth Barrett to Mr. Boyd | UNPUBLISHED LETTERS OF | ELIZABETH BARRETT BROWNING | TO HUGH STUART BOYD | [*seal lettered Hope End*] | INTRODUCED AND EDITED BY BARBARA P. McCARTHY | PUBLISHED FOR WELLESLEY COLLEGE BY | YALE UNIVERSITY PRESS· NEW HAVEN· 1955

Collation: 23.5 × 15.4 cm; [Unsigned 1^8 $2–10^{16}$ 11^{12} 12^8]; 172 leaves.

Pagination: [2] [i–v] vi–xxxix [xl], [1–2] 3–289 [290] 291–299 [300] [2].

Binding: Red calico (V) cloth. No stamping on sides. Running down the spine: 'McCARTHY: Elizabeth Barrett to Mr. Boyd | YALE.' White wove end papers. Ten stab holes at inner margin. All edges trimmed.

D36 : Letters to George Barrett 1958

[*in white on black background*] LETTERS | OF THE | BROWN-INGS | TO | GEORGE | BARRETT | [*in black over a facsimile of a letter from R.B. to G.B.*] EDITED BY PAUL LANDIS WITH THE ASSISTANCE OF RONALD E. FREEMAN | UNIVERSITY OF ILLINOIS PRESS, URBANA, 1958.

Collation: 22.9 × 15.3 cm; [Unsigned $1–2^{16}$ 3^{10} $4–13^{16}$]; 202 leaves.

Pagination: [i–x], [1] 2–34 [35] 36–264 [265–266] 267–333 [334–335] 336–340 [341] 342–348 [349] 350–354 [355] 356–361 [362] 363–366 [367] 368–370 [371] 372–374 [375] 376–392 [2].

Binding: Gray buckram. Front stamped in brown with a design of letter sheets on which is printed 'LETTERS | OF THE | BROWNINGS | TO | GEORGE | BARRETT.' Back blank. Spine: 'LANDIS | [*running down the spine:*] LETTERS OF THE BROWNINGS TO GEORGE BARRETT | UNIVERSITY OF ILLINOIS PRESS' All stamped in brown. Brown end papers. Twelve stab holes at inner margin. All edges trimmed.

D37 : Elizabeth Barrett and R. Shelton Mackenzie, ed. David Bonnell Green, *Studies in Bibliography*, XIV (1961), 245.

REPRINTS

E

E1 : **A Child's Grave at Florence** [London, 1850?].
Copy MH

E2 : **Poems** . . . With an Essay by Henry T. Tuckerman. New York,
C. S. Francis; Boston, J. H. Francis, 1850. 2 V.
Copies DLC MB ViU

E3 : **Prometheus Bound, and Other Poems;** Including Sonnets
from the Portuguese, Casa Guidi Windows, etc. New York, C. S.
Francis and Co.; Boston, J. H. Francis and Co., 1851.
Copies TxWB MH CtY

E4 : **Poems** . . . New York, C. S. Francis and Co.; Boston, Crosby
and Nichols, 1852. 2 V.
Copies MH NcD MBat

E5 : Entry cancelled.

E6 : **Prometheus Bound, and Other Poems;** Including Sonnets
from the Portuguese, Casa Guidi Windows, etc. New York, C. S.
Francis and Co.; Boston, J. H. Francis and Co., 1852.
Copies MB NjP Cty

E7 : **Poems** . . . With an Introductory Essay by Henry T. Tuckerman. New York, C. S. Francis & Co., Boston Crosby & Nichols,
1853. 2 V.
Copies CtY PP MiU

E8 : **Poems** . . . With an Introductory Essay by Henry T. Tuckerman. New York, C. S. Francis and Co.; Boston, Crosby and Nichols,
1853, 2 V. in 1.
Copy CtY

E9 : **Poems** . . . With an Introductory Essay by Henry T. Tuckerman. New York, C. S. Francis and Co.; Boston, Crosby and Nichols,
1854. 2 V.
Copies MH CtY L NjP

E10 : **Prometheus Bound and Other Poems;** Including Sonnets
from the Portuguese, Casa Guidi Windows, etc. New York, C. S.
Francis and Co.; Boston, J. H. Francis and Co., 1854.
Copies CtY NIC MH

E11 : **Prometheus Bound and Other Poems;** Including Sonnets
from the Portuguese, Casa Guidi Windows, etc. New York, C. S.
Francis and Co.; Boston, J. H. Francis, 1856.
Copies MH NjP MBat

E12 : **Aurora Leigh.** Second edition, London, Chapman and Hall,
1857.
Copies CtY MWelC L

E13 : **Aurora Leigh.** Third Edition. London, Chapman and Hall, 1857.
Copies Liv Le

E14 : **Poems** . . . New York, C. S. Francis and Co., 1857. 2 V.
Copies DLC TU NjP

E15 : **Poems** . . . New Edition. New York, C. S. Francis and Co., 1858. 2 V.
Copies CtY MH NCU

E16 : **Aurora Leigh.** New York, Boston, C. S. Francis and Co., 1859.
Copies DLC MH MWelC

E17 : **Poems** . . . New York, C. S. Francis and Co., 1859. 3 V.
Copies MH NN MB

E18 : **Aurora Leigh.** Fifth Edition. London, Chapman and Hall, 1860.
Copies IU L O

E19 : **Aurora Leigh.** New York, Boston, C. S. Francis and Co., 1860.
Copies MH MB

E20 : **Poems.** New Edition. New York, C. S. Francis and Co., 1860. 2 V.
Copies MH MWelC ViU

E21 : **Poetical Works.** New York, James Miller, 1860.
Copy PU

E22 : **Aurora Leigh,** and Other Poems. New York, James Miller [1861].
Copies ViU OO OCL

E23 : **Only a Curl.** [Baltimore, 1861] Privately Printed, James H. Stone.
Copy CSmH

E23.1 : **Poems.** New York, Charles S. Francis, 1861. 2V
Copy MH

E24 : **Aurora Leigh,** and other poems. New York, James Miller, 1862.
Copies MH CtY

E25 : **Last Poems.** Second Edition. London, Chapman and Hall, 1862.
Copies CU L

E26 : Last Poems. With a Memorial by Theodore Tilton. New York, James Miller, 1862.
Copies DLC MB TxWB

E27 : Poems . . . Fifth Edition. London, Chapman and Hall, 1862. 3 V.
Copies IU CtY L

E28 : Poems . . . With an Introductory Essay by Henry T. Tuckerman. New York, James Miller, 1862. 3 V.
Copies MH NJP PPL

E29 : [Works]. New York, James Miller [1862–63]. 5 V. (Blue and Gold Series).
Copies NN CtY TxWB

E30 : Aurora Leigh, and Other Poems. New York, James Miller, 1863.
Copy ViU

E31 : Essays on the Greek Christian Poets and the English Poets. New York, James Miller, 1863.
Copies MH DLC MB

E32 : Last Poems. With a Memorial by Theodore Tilton. New York, James Miller, 1863.
Copies ViU PPL IU

E33 : Poems . . . New York, James Miller, 1863. 4 V.
Copies NJP MWelC WaU CU

E34 : Aurora Leigh. Sixth Edition. London, Chapman and Hall, 1864.
Copies MH WB

E35 : Aurora Leigh, and Other Poems. New York, James Miller, 1864.
Copy IU

E36 : Essays on the Greek Christian Poets and the English Poets. New York, James Miller, 1864.
Copy ICU

E37 : Last Poems. With a Memorial by Theodore Tilton. New York, James Miller, 1864.
Copies MA NJP NCU

E38 : Poems. Sixth Edition. London, Chapman and Hall, 1864. 3 V.
Copies TxWB IU L

E39 : Poems... New York, James Miller, 1864. 3 V.
Copies ICU MOU CtY

E40 : Poems. A New Edition. Boston, Ticknor and Fields, 1864. 4
V. (Author's Edition).
Copy OCU (Cited National Union Catalogue. *Not seen*).

E41 : Aurora Leigh, and Other Poems. New York, James Miller,
1865.
Copies MH ICRL

E42 : Poems of the Intellect and the Affections. Philadelphia, E.
H. Butler, 1865.
Copies MWelC NN CtY

E43 : Aurora Leigh. Eighth Edition. London, Chapman and Hall,
1866.
Copy OB

E44 : Aurora Leigh, and Other Poems. New York, James Miller,
1866.
Copies MH OCLW

E45 : Essays on the Greek Christian Poets and the English Poets.
New York, James Miller, 1866.
Copy DLC

E46 : Entry cancelled.

E47 : Entry cancelled.

E48 : Poems... New York, James Miller, 1866. 4 V.
Copies PU OCl

E49 : A Selection from the Poetry of Elizabeth Barrett Browning.
London, Chapman and Hall, 1866.
Copies TxWB ViU MH C [Proof sheets corrected by R. B. at TxU]

E50 : A Selection from the Poetry of Elizabeth Barrett Browning.
Second Edition. London, Chapman and Hall, 1866.
Copies MH L MWelC

E51 : Aurora Leigh, and Other Poems. New York, James Miller,
1867.
Copies IU OO

E52 : Poems of Childhood ... New York, James Miller, 1867.
Copies MB NN DLC L

E53 : Poems... New York, James Miller, 1867. 3 V.
Copy ICU

E54 : The Poetical Works . . . New York, James Miller [1867?]. 2 V. in 1. (*Household Edition*).
Copy OCU

E55 : Works . . . New York, James Miller, 1867. 5 V. (Blue and Gold Series).
Copies ViU OUW

E56 : Poems of the Intellect and the Affections . . . Philadelphia, E. H. Butler and Co., 1868.
Copies NN NCM

E57 : The True Mary: Being Mrs. Browning's Poem, "The Virgin Mary to the Child Jesus." Edited by W. A. Muhlenberg. New York, Thomas Whittaker, 1868.
Copies MH NNU CtY L

E58 : Aurora Leigh, and Other Poems. New York, James Miller [1869?].
Copies MH DLC CU

E59 : Entry cancelled.

E60 : Poems. Complete . . . With an Introductory Essay by Henry T. Tuckerman. New York, James Miller, 1869. 3 V.
Copies IaU OCL MH

E60.1 : Poetical Works . . . Seventh Edition. London, Smith, Elder, and Co., 1870. 5 V.
Copy MdBJ

E61 : Aurora Leigh. Tenth Edition. London, Smith, Elder, and Co., 1870.
Listed English Catalogue. *Not seen.*

E62 : Lady Geraldine's Courtship. New York, Charles Scribner and Co., 1870.
Copies MH MB DLC

E63 : Poems of the Intellect and the Affections. Philadelphia, E. H. Butler and Co., 1870.
Copies IU KAStB CtY

E64 : Poetical Works . . . Eighth Edition. London, Smith, Elder, and Co., 1870. 5 V.
Copy MdBJ

E65 : Poetical Works . . . New York, James Miller [1870]. (Florence Edition).
Copies MH NN CtY

E66 : Poetical Works . . . Complete in One Volume. New York, Hurst and Co. [1870?].
Copies IU FU ViU ARU

E67 : Poetical Works . . . New York, T. Y. Crowell [1870] (Florence Edition).
Copy WaU

E68 : The True Mary, Being Mrs. Browning's poem, "The Virgin Mary to the Child Jesus." Edited by W. A. Muhlenberg. Second Edition. New York, Thomas Whittaker, 1870.
Copy KyU

E69 : Poetical Works . . . Ninth Edition. London, Smith, Elder, and Co., 1871–72. 5 V.
Copy MH

E70 : Poetical Works . . . New York, James Miller, 1871. 2 V. in 1.
Copies MB MH L

E71 : Poetical Works . . . New York, James Miller, 1871. (Diamond Edition).
Copies MH NRU

E72 : Poetical Works . . . Boston, Fields, Osgood, and Co., 1871, (Diamond Edition).
Copies MH NIC ViU

E73 : A Selection from the Poetry of Elizabeth Barrett Browning. Third Edition. London, Smith, Elder. and Co., 1871.
Copies DLC MH

E74 : Aurora Leigh, and Other Poems. New York, James Miller, 1872.
Copy MH

E75 : Aurora Leigh, and Other Poems. New York, James Miller, 1872. (Diamond Edition).
Copy MH

E76 : Aurora Leigh. Copyright Edition. Leipzig, B. Tauchnitz, 1872.
Copies MH DLC L

E77 : Poems of Memory and Hope. New York, James Miller, 1872.
Copies NCAS DLC

E78 : Poetical Works . . . Boston, J. R. Osgood and Co., 1872. (Diamond Edition).
Copy MH

E79 : **Rhyme of the Duchess May.** Low, 1872. Listed English Catalogue. *Not seen.*

E80 : **A Selection from the Poetry of Elizabeth Barrett Browning.** First Series. Fourth Edition. London, Smith, Elder, and Co., 1872. Copies NN LU

E81 : **A Selection from the Poetry of Elizabeth Barrett Browning.** Copyright Edition ... Leipzig, B. Tauchnitz, 1872. Copies DLC MB

E82 : **Aurora Leigh.** Thirteenth Edition. London, 1873. Copy E (not seen)

E83 : **Lady Geraldine's Courtship.** New York, James Miller, 1873. Copy MH

E84 : **Poems** ... New York, James Miller, 1873. 3 V. Copy RPB

E85 : **Poems of Memory and Hope,** etc. New York, James Miller, 1873. Copy L

E86 : **Poems of the Intellect and the Affections.** Philadelphia, Hubbard Brothers, 1873. Copy DLC

E87 : **Poetical Works** ... Tenth Edition. London, Smith, Elder, and Co., 1873. 5 V. Copies DLC MH NN CtY

E88 : **The Rhyme of the Duchess May.** London, S. Low, Marston, Low, and Searle, 1873. Copies IU L

E89 : **Aurora Leigh.** New York, James Miller, 1874. Copy PSC

E90 : **Aurora Leigh, and Other Poems.** New York, James Miller, 1874. (Diamond Edition). Copies IU DLC

E91 : **Poems.** New York, James Miller, 1874. 3 V. Copies MH RPB

E92 : **Poetical Works** ... Complete in One Volume. New York, James Miller, 1874. Copy RPB

E93 : **Lady Geraldine's Courtship.** Boston, Houghton, Mifflin and Co., 1875.
Copy MB

E94 : **Poetical Works.** New York, James Miller, 1875.
Copies IU MH OClW

E95 : **Aurora Leigh.** Fourteenth Edition. London, Smith, Elder, and Co., 1876.
Copy C-Vu

E96 : **Lady Geraldine's Courtship.** New York, James Miller, 1876.
Copy PU

E97 : **Lady Geraldine's Courtship.** Boston, J. R. Osgood and Co., 1876. (Vest Pocket Series).
Copies MB MH CU L

E98 : **The Poetical Works** . . . Complete. New York, James Miller, 1876. 2 V. (Household Edition).
Copies NN WU

E99 : **Aurora Leigh.** New York, James Miller, 1877.
Copies MH NN MWelC

E100 : **The Earlier Poems of Elizabeth Barrett Browning, 1826–1833.** Edited by R. H. Shepherd. London, Bartholomew Robson, 1878. [1877].
Copies L O NjP CtY TxU

E101 : **Mrs. E. B. Browning's Letters and Essays.** With a memoir by R. H. Stoddard. In two volumes. New York, James Miller [1877]. Vol. 1 t.p. Letters to Richard Hengist Horne. Vol. 2 t.p. The Book of the Poets. Some Account of the Greek Christian Poets.
Copies DLC NIC MiU L

E102 : **Life, Letters, and Essays of Elizabeth Barrett Browning.** New York, J. W. Lovell [1877?] 2 Vols. Vol. 1, t.p. Letters to R. H. Horne; Vol. 2 t.p. Essays on the English Poets and the Greek Christian Poets.
Copies PST MDU

E103 : **Life, Letters, and Essays of Elizabeth Barrett Browning.** With a preface and memoir by Richard Henry Stoddard. New York, T. R. Knox and Co. [c 1877]. 2 V.
Copies TJU MBU

E104 : **Poetical Works** . . . Eleventh Edition. London, Smith, Elder, and Co., 1877. 5 V.
Copies MH MWelC

E105 : Poetical Works . . . New York, Hurst and Co. [1877].
Copy IU

E106 : Poetical Works . . . New York, James Miller, 1877.
Copy L

E107 : Poetical Works . . . New York, James Miller, 1877. 4 V.
Copies MH MWelC NRU

E108 : Poetical Works . . . New York, Syndicate Trading Co.
[1877?].
Copy NSyU

E109 : A Selection from the Poetry of Elizabeth Barrett Browning.
Seventh Edition. London, Smith, Elder, and Co., 1877.
Copy L

E110 : Earlier Poems. 1826–1833. Now First Printed in America.
New York, James Miller, 1878.
Copies MB MH CtY

E111 : The Earlier Poems of Elizabeth Barrett Browning, 1826–
1833. New York, J. W. Lovell [1878?].
Copy CtY

E112 : Poems . . . New York, J. W. Lovell and Co., 1878. 5 V.
Copy MDU

E113 : Poems . . . New York, James Miller, 1879. 2 V. in 1.
Copy TxWB

E114 : A Selection from the Poetry of Elizabeth Barrett Browning.
Ninth Edition. London, Smith, Elder, and Co., 1879.
Copy TxWB

E115 : Poetical Works . . . New York, James Miller, 1879. 4 V.
Copies CtY CDU

E116 : Poetical Works . . . New York, James Miller [187–]. 2 V. in 1.
(New York Edition).
Copies MH CLU-C NJP

E117 : Poetical Works . . . New York, Worthington [187–] (Household Edition).
Copy ViU

E118 : He Giveth His Beloved Sleep. Boston, Lee and Shepard
[c 1880].
Copies LU ViU

E119 : **Poems of the Intellect and the Affections.** Philadelphia, Burlock and Co., 1880.
Copy CtY (cited Yale Catalogue. *Not seen.*)

E120 : **Poetical Works . . .** Twelfth Edition. London, Smith, Elder, and Co., 1880. 5 V.
Copies CLU-C C

E121 : **Poetical Works . . .** New York, James Miller [c 1880].
Copy L

E122 : **Poetical Works.** Chicago, Belford, Clarke and Co. [1880?].
Copies L MH OCl

E123 : **A Selection from the Poetry of Elizabeth Barrett Browning.** Second Series. London, Smith, Elder, and Co., 1880.
Copies L MWelC MB

E124 : **A Selection from the Poetry . . .** Second Series. Second Edition. London, Smith, Elder, and Co., 1880.
Copies ViU LU

E125 : **A Selection from the Poetry of Elizabeth Barrett Browning.** First Series. Tenth Edition, Smith, Elder, and Co., 1880.
Copies MWelC MB

E126 : **A Selection from the Poetry of Elizabeth Barrett Browning.** First Series. Eleventh Edition. London, Smith, Elder, and Co., 1880.
Copy ViU

E127 : **Lady Geraldine's Courtship,** Boston, Houghton, Mifflin and Co., 1881.
Copies MB MH

E128 : **Aurora Leigh.** Seventeenth Edition. London, Smith, Elder, and Co., 1882.
Copy TxU

E129 : **He Giveth His Beloved Sleep.** Boston, Lee and Shepard; New York, C. T. Dillingham, 1882.
Copies DLC ViU MH

E130 : . . . **Lady Geraldine's Courtship.** Boston, Houghton, Mifflin and Co., 1882.
Copy MA

E131 : **Mrs. Browning's Birthday Book.** Edited by R. H. Stoddard. New York, James Miller, 1882.
Copies OCl DLC L

E132 : Poetical Works . . . New York, Thomas Y. Crowell and Co. [1882].
Copies DLC MB MiU

E133 : Poetical Works . . . New York, Thomas Y. Crowell and Co. [1882]. ⟨a different edition from the above⟩
Copies CtY IU MH

E134 : A Selection from the Poetry of Elizabeth Barrett Browning. First Series. Twelfth Edition. London, Smith, Elder, and Co., 1882.
Copy CLU-C

E135 : A Selection from the Poetry of Elizabeth Barrett Browning. Second Series. Third Edition. London, Smith, Elder, and Co., 1882.
Copy CLU-C

E136 : Aurora Leigh. Eighteenth Edition. London, Smith, Elder, and Co., 1883.
Copy CLU-C

E137 : Aurora Leigh. New York, Thomas Y. Crowell and Co. [1883].
Copies IU DLC MH

E138 : Poetical Works . . . Thirteenth Edition. London, Smith, Elder, and Co., 1883. 5 V.
Copy LU

E139 : Poetical Works . . . New York, John B. Alden, 1883.
Copies ViU CaOTU

E140 : A Selection from the Poetry . . . Thirteenth Edition. London, Smith, Elder, and Co., 1883.
Copy Le

E141 : Aurora Leigh. From the Twelfth London Edition. New York, Thomas Y. Crowell and Co. [c 1884].
Copy MH

E142 : Aurora Leigh . . . New York, J. W. Lovell Co. [1884].
Copy DLC

E143 : Poems of the Intellect and the Affections . . . Philadelphia, Hubbard Bros., 1884.
Copies CtY OO

E144 : Poetical Works . . . New York, Worthington, 1884.
Copy ICU

E144.1 : Poetical Works . . . New York, Dodd, Mead, and Company, 1884.
Copies TxU PP CSmH

E145 : A Selection from the Poetry of Elizabeth Barrett Browning.
New Edition. London, Smith, Elder, and Co., 1884. 2 V.
Copies MiU TxWB

E146 : A Selection from the Poetry of Elizabeth Barrett Browning.
First Series. New Edition. New York, Macmillan and Co., 1884.
Copies CtY MH ViU

E147 : A Selection from the Poetry of Elizabeth Barrett Browning.
Second Series. New Edition. New York, Macmillan and Co., 1884.
Copy MH

E148 : Lady Geraldine's Courtship. Boston, Lee and Shepard; New York, C. T. Dillingham, 1885.
Copies DLC NCU

E149 : Poetical Works . . . New York, Dodd, Mead, and Co., 1885. 5 V.
Copies MH MB

E150 : Poems . . . New York, T. R. Knox, 1885. 5 V.
Copies IU NN KyU

E151 : Poetical Works . . . Fourteenth Edition. London, Smith, Elder, and Co., 1886. 5 V.
Copies NN CST TxWB

E152 : Poetical Works . . . New York, Dodd, Mead, and Co., 1886. 5 V.
Copy MB

E153 : Poetical Works . . . New York, T. Y. Crowell and Co. [1886]. (Astor Edition).
Copies IU NN MiU

E154 : Poetical Works . . . New York, Thomas Y. Crowell and Co. [c 1886].
Copies PBL NBU MH

E155 : Poetical Works . . . Troy, Nims Knight, [1886].
Copy PV

E156 : A Selection from the Poetry of Elizabeth Barrett Browning.
New Edition. London, Smith, Elder, and Co., 1886. 2 V.
Copy TxWB

E157 : **Sonnets from the Portuguese.** Boston, Ticknor and Co. [cop. 1886] ⟨First separate edition⟩.
Copies TxU MH NN TxWB

E158 : **Sonnets from the Portuguese.** Edited with notes by W. J. Rolfe. Boston, D. Lathrop and Co. [c. 1886].
Copies MWelC CtY DLC MH

E159 : **Aurora Leigh.** Nineteenth Edition. London, Smith, Elder, and Co., 1887.
Copy Le

E160 : **Aurora Leigh.** Twentieth Edition. London, Smith, Elder, and Co., 1887.
Copy L

E161 : **Poems** ... With a Prefatory Note by Robert Browning. London, Smith, Elder, and Co., 1887.
Copy L

E162 : **Poems** ... London, Smith, Elder, and Co., 1887.
Copies DLC NJP MH L

E163 : **Works** . . . New York, Thomas Y. Crowell and Co.[1887].
Copies NN MoU IEN

E164 : **Romances, Lyrics and Sonnets from the Poetic Works of Elizabeth Barrett Browning.** Boston & New York, Houghton, Mifflin, and Co., 1888.
Copies MH PSC MB

E165 : **The Seraphim; and other poems** . . . London, New York; Ward, Lock, and Co. [1888].
Copy L

E166 : **From Queens' Gardens.** Selected Poems of Elizabeth Barrett Browning . . . Gathered by Rose Porter. Troy, New York, Nims and Knight, 1889.
Copies DLC CtY

E167 : **Life, Letters, and Essays** . . . New York, Worthington, 1889. 2 V. Vol. 1. t.p. Letters . . . Addressed to Richard Hengist Horne. Vol. 2. t.p. Essays on the English Poets and the Greek Christian Poets.
Copies PBL TxU MH (V2.)

E168 : **Poems** ... New York, Worthington, 1889. 5 V.
Copy MH

E169 : **Poetical Works.** With a Prefatory Note by Robert Browning
... London, Smith, Elder, and Co., 1889–90. 6 V.
Copies L MH CtY O

E170 : **Poems** . . . London, George Routledge and Sons, 1887.
(Routledge's Pocket Library).
Copies CtY L

E171 : **Poems** . . . London, George Routledge and Sons, 1887.
Copies CtY NBUG L

E172 : **Poems.** Selected and Arranged by Robert Browning. New
York, Thomas Y. Crowell [1887].
Copies MH NN COU IEN

E173 : **Poetical Works** . . . From 1826 to 1844. Edited with a Memoir by J. H. Ingram. London, Ward, Lock, and Co. [1887]. (People's Standard Library).
Copies L O

E174 : **Poetical Works** . . . London, Ward, Lock, and Co. [1887].
(People's Standard Library).
Copies L DCU

E175 : **Poetical Works** . . . New York, A. L. Burt Co., 1887. (The
Home Library).
Copies PP OClW

E176 : **Poetical Works** . . . Troy, N.Y., Nims and Knight, 1887.
Copies DLC IU

E177 : **Sonnets from the Portuguese.** Boston, Ticknor and Co.
[1887].
Copy L

E178 : **The Mrs. Browning Birthday Book.** With a Preface by the
Rev. Charles Mackeson. London, Griffith, Farran, and Co. [1889].
Copy L

E179 : **Poetical Works** . . . New York, T. R. Knox and Co. [188–].
2 V. in 1. (Household Edition).
Copy MH

E180 : **Poetical Works.** With an introductory essay by Henry T.
Tuckerman. New York, T. R. Knox [188–]. 3 V.
Copies MH ViU

E181 : **Poetical Works** . . . New York, Hurst and Co., [188–].
Copies DLC MH ARU

E181.1 : Poetical Works . . . London, Smith, Elder, and Co., 1889–1890. 6 V.
Copies MH L

E182 : Aurora Leigh. London, Smith, Elder, and Co., 1890.
Copy CU

E183 : Aurora Leigh. Popular Edition. New York, Universal Publishing Co. [1890].
Copy IU

E184 : Aurora Leigh, a Poem. New York, Worthington Co., 1890.
Copies DLC PP ViU GEU

E185 : Mrs. Browning's Birthday Book. Edited by R. H. Stoddard. New York, Worthington, 1890.
Copy TxWB

E186 : Poetical Works . . . Griffith, 1890. Listed English Catalogue. *Not seen.*

E187 : Poetical Works . . . New York, Worthington, 1890. 3 V.
Copies GEU TNJ NCU

E188 : Romances, Lyrics and Sonnets from the Poetic Works of Elizabeth Barrett Browning. Boston, etc., Houghton, Mifflin, and Co., 1890.
Copies FU MH

E189 : Sonnets from the Portuguese. New York, London, G. P. Putnam's Sons [1890]. (Literary Gems).
Copies MH MB

E190 : Aurora Leigh. Smith, 1891. Listed English Catalogue. *Not seen.*

E191 : The Battle of Marathon. Introduction by H. Buxton Forman. Reprinted in type-facsimile. London, 1891.
Copies MH TxU L

E192 : Mrs. Browning's Birthday Book. Edited by R. H. Stoddard. New York, Worthington, 1891.
Copy TxWB

E193 : Poetical Works . . . New York, Thomas Y. Crowell and Co. [c 1891].
Copies FU DLC

E194 : Poetical Works . . . From 1826 to 1844. London and Sydney. Griffith, Farran, and Co. [1891]. (Newbery Classics).
Copies L O

E195 : Sonnets from the Portuguese. London, Ernest Nister; New York, E. P. Dutton and Co., 1891. (Laurel Wreath Series).
Copy L

E196 : A Selection from the Poetry of Elizabeth Barrett Browning. First—(Second) Series. New Edition. London, Smith, Elder, and Co., 1891–92. 2 V.
Copies IU WaSpG (Vol. 1)

E197 : Aurora Leigh and Other Poems. Vignette Edition. New York. Frederick A. Stokes Co., 1892.
Copies DLC NN PPD

E198 : Mrs. Browning's Birthday Book. Edited by R. H. Stoddard. New York, Worthington, 1892.
Copies RPB TxWB

E199 : A Book of Modern Ballads. By E. B. Browning . . . and others. London, Hildesheimer and Faulkner, New York, G. C. Whitney [1892].
Copies IU O

E200 : Poems . . . Selected and Arranged by Mr. Robert Browning. London, Smith, Elder, and Co., 1892.
Copies DLC NN L

E201 : Poems . . . London, F. Warne and Co., 1892. (Albion Edition).
Copies O DT

E202 : Poems . . . New York, Frederick A. Stokes Co., 1892. (Vignette Edition).
Copies DLC MH CLSU

E203 : Poetical Works . . . New York, Dodd, Mead, and Co., 1892. 5 V.
Copies ViU NNC NCU IEN

E204 : Poetical Works . . . New York, Worthington, 1892.
Copy IU

E205 : Aurora Leigh. New York, Dodd, Mead, and Co. [1893]. (Giunta Series).
Copy OCU

E206 : Poems. Simpkin, 1893. Listed English Catalogue. *Not seen.*

E207 : Poems . . . Selected and Arranged by Robert Browning. London, Smith, Elder, and Co., 1893.
Copy CtY

E208 : **Poems** . . . Selected and Arranged by Robert Browning. New York, Thomas Y. Crowell and Co. [c 1893].
Copies ViU DLC MH

E209 : **Poems** . . . London, F. Warne and Co., 1893. (Albion Edition).
Copies MH L

E210 : **Romances, Lyrics and Sonnets from the Poetic Works of Elizabeth Barrett Browning.** Boston, New York, Houghton, Mifflin and Co., 1893.
Copy CtY

E211 : **Aurora Leigh; a Poem.** New York, The H. W. Hagemann Co., 1894.
Copy MH

E212 : **Poems** . . . London and New York, F. Warne and Co., 1894. (Albion Edition).
Copies MH PP ViU

E213 : **Sonnets from the Portuguese.** Introduction by Edmund Gosse. London, J. M. Dent and Co., 1894.
Copies TxU FU TxWB L

E214 : **Poetical Works** . . . With an introductory essay by Henry T. Tuckerman. New York, Frederick A. Stokes Co. [1895]. 3 V.
Copies IU CtY DLC

E215 : **Entry Cancelled.**

E216 : **The Brownings for the Young.** Edited by Frederic G. Kenyon. London, Smith, Elder, and Co.; New York, Macmillan and Co., 1896.
Copies DLC OCl L O

E217 : **Poems.** Routledge, 1896. Listed English Catalogue. *Not seen.*

E218 : **Poetical Works** . . . New York, Dodd, Mead, and Co., 1896. 5 V.
Copies IU OO GU

E219 : **Prometheus Bound and Other Poems** . . . With an introduction by Alice Meynell. London, Ward, Lock and Co., 1896. (XIXth Century Classics).
Copies MWelC KU CU L O

E220 : **Sonnets from the Portuguese.** Boston, Copeland and Day, 1896.
Copies DLC ViU MH L

E221 : **Letters of Elizabeth Barrett Browning.** Edited with Biographical Additions by F. G. Kenyon. Second Edition. London, Smith, Elder, and Co., 1897. 2 V.
Copy MH

E222 : **The Letters of Elizabeth Barrett Browning.** Edited with Biographical Additions by F. G. Kenyon. New York, The Macmillan Co.; London, Macmillan and Co., ltd., 1897. 2 V.
Copies DLC MB MH

E223 : **Poetical Works** . . . Edited by Sir Frederic G. Kenyon. London, Smith, Elder, and Co., 1897.
Copies MB OCU L MH O

E224 : **Poems.** Warne, 1897. Listed English Catalogue. *Not seen.*

E225 : **Poetical Works** . . . New York, Macmillan and Co., 1897.
Copies CtY PP MWelC

E226 : **Sonnets from the Portuguese.** [London, Ballantyne Press, 1897].
Copies CU CSmH

E227 : **Sonnets from the Portuguese.** [London, Hacon and Ricketts, 1897].
Copies CLU-C MH PSC L

E228 : **Sonnets from the Portuguese.** [Edinburgh, Privately printed, Phoebe Anna Traquair, 1897].
Copies CSmH MH INU

E229 : **Sonnets from the Portuguese.** [London, Vale Press, 1897].
Copy LU

E230 : **Sonnets from the Portuguese.** Portland, Maine, [First Edition] T. B. Mosher, 1897. Old World Series.
Copies MB MH CtY

E231 : **Aurora Leigh.** New Edition with Prefatory Note by A. C. Swinburne. London, Smith, Elder, and Co., 1898.
Copies MH CtY L

E232 : **Letters of Robert Browning and Elizabeth Barrett Barrett, 1845–1846.** London and New York, Harper and Brothers, 1898. 2 V.
Copies TxU ODU

E233 : **Letters of Elizabeth Barrett Browning.** Edited by F. G. Kenyon. Third Edition. London, Smith, Elder, and Co., 1898. 2 V.
Copies MH NIC DLC

E234 : The Letters of Elizabeth Barrett Browning. Edited with Biographical Additions by F. G. Kenyon. New York, the Macmillan Co.; London, Macmillan and Co., ltd., 1898. 2 V.
Copies DLC ViU MB

E235 : The letters of Elizabeth Barrett Browning. Edited with Biographical Additions by F. G. Kenyon. Fourth Edition. London, The Macmillan Co., 1898. 2 V.
Copies MWelC MiU TxWB

E236 : Selected Poems. With Biographical Sketch and Notes. New York, Effingham Maynard & Co., 1898. [cop. 1887]. (English Classics Series, 64.)
Copies MiU MH

E237 : Sonnets . . . Guildford, A. C. Curtis, 1898.
Copy DLC

E238 : Sonnets from the Portuguese. Portland, Maine, T. B. Mosher [Second Edition]. 1898. Old World Series.
Copy DLC

E239 : Sonnets from the Portuguese. London, George Bell and Sons, 1898.
Copies MH DLC IU L O

E240 : Sonnets from the Portuguese. [East Aurora, N.Y., The Roycroft Shop, 1898].
Copies DLC CtY MB

E241 : Sonnets from the Portuguese. [Oxford, 1898].
Copy O

E242 : Aurora Leigh with an introductory note by E. W. Rinder. London, Walter Scott, limited [1899]. (The Canterbury Poets).
Copies DLC L MH

E243 : Aurora Leigh. Edited by H. Buxton Forman. London, J. M. Dent and Co., 1899. (The Temple Classics).
Copies MH CtY L

E244 : The Letters of Robert Browning and Elizabeth Barrett Barrett 1845–1846. Edited by Robert Wiedemann Barrett Browning. New York and London, Harper and Brothers, 1899. 2 V.
Copies IU CtY CLU-C

E245 : The letters of Elizabeth Barrett Browning. Edited with Biographical Additions by F. G. Kenyon . . . (New Edition). New York, The Macmillan Co.; London, Macmillan and Co., ltd., 1899. 2 V. in 1.
Copies DLC MH

E246 : **Lord Walter's Wife.** Wausau, Wisconsin, The Philosopher Press, 1899.
Copies DLC TxWB

E247 : **Poetical Works** . . . New York, Dodd, Mead, and Co., 1899. 5 V.
Copies ViU TxWB

E248 : **Poetical Works** . . . New York, The Macmillan Co., 1899.
Copies ViU GEU

E249 : **Poems.** Routledge, 1899. Listed English Catalogue. *Not seen.*

E250 : **Sonnets from the Portuguese.** With an Introduction by F. W. Gunsaulus. Chicago, R. F. Seymour [1899].
Copies DLC TxU ICN CtY

E251 : **Poems.** Selected and Arranged by Robert Browning. Boston, J. Knight Co. [189-].
Copy MH

E252 : **Poetical Works** . . . New York, The American News Co. [189-].
Copy MH

E253 : **Sonnets from the Portuguese.** London, G. G. Harrap and Co. [189-]. (The King's Treasury of Literary Masterpieces).
Copy NN (Cited National Union Catalogue. *Not seen.*)

E254 : **Sonnets from the Portuguese.** New York, London, G. P. Putnam's Sons [189-].
Copies DLC MB MH

E255 : **Aurora Leigh.** With a Prefatory Note by Algernon Charles Swinburne. New Edition. London, Smith, Elder, and Co., 1900.
Copy WU

E256 : **Aurora Leigh.** With Introduction by Charlotte Porter and Helen A. Clarke. New York, Thomas Y. Crowell and Co. [c 1900].
Copies MH NIC NN

E257 : **Beautiful Thoughts from Robert and Elizabeth Browning,** arranged by Margaret Shipp. New York, J. Pott and Co., 1900.
Copy DLC

E258 : **The Complete Poetical Works** . . . Edited by Harriet Waters Preston. Boston and New York, Houghton, Mifflin Co., 1900. (Cambridge Edition of the Poets).
Copies MH L DLC MB

E259 : Complete Works . . . Edited with Introductions and Notes by Charlotte Porter and Helen A. Clarke . . . N.Y., T. Y. Crowell and Co. [1900]. 6 V.
Copies PPT MiU TU

E260 : Poetical Works . . . London, Smith, Elder, and Co., 1900.
Copy CSt

E261 : Poetical Works . . . New York, the Macmillan Co., 1900.
Copies MH ORU

E262 : Poetical Works . . . New York, Dodd, Mead, and Co., 1900. 5 V.
Copies ViU PP

E263 : Complete Works . . . New York, E. R. Dumont [c 1900]. 6 V.
Copies COU IEN

E264 : Complete Works . . . New York, Society of English and French Literature [c 1900].
Copies GEU IdU

E265 : Complete Works . . . Edited by Charlotte Porter and Helen A. Clarke. New York, Fred De Fau and Co. [c 1900]. 6 V.
Copies OC KyMoreT

E266 : Poetical Works . . . With an Introduction by Alice Meynell. London, Ward, Lock, and Co. [c 1900].
Copy Liv

E267 : Sonnets from the Portuguese . . . London, G. G. Harrap and Co. [1900?]. (Sesame Booklets, no. 21).
Copy MiU

E268 : Sonnets from the Portuguese. London, George Bell and Sons, 1900.
Copy MH

E269 : Sonnets from the Portuguese. New York and Boston, H. M. Caldwell Co. [1900].
Copies DLC ViU TxWB

E270 : . . . Sonnets from the Portuguese. Preface by Edmund Gosse. Portland, Maine, Thomas B. Mosher, 1900. [First Edition]. Vest Pocket Series.
Copies MH NN PU CtY

E271 : Sonnets from the Portuguese. Preface by Edmund Gosse. Aiken, S.C., The Palmetto Press, 1900.
Copies DLC NN ICN CtY

E272 : Sonnets from the Portuguese. [New Rochelle, N.Y.] Elston Press [1900].
Copies TxWB DLC CSmH CtY

E273 : Casa Guidi Windows. With Introduction by A. M. F. Robinson. London and New York, John Lane, 1901.
Copies IaU MB L

E274 : Complete Works . . . Edited by Charlotte Porter and Helen A. Clarke. New York, George D. Sproul, 1901. 6 V. (Autograph Edition) WU TxU; (Arno Edition) NNC CST TxWB; (Connoisseur's Edition) NBU.

E274.1 : Poems of Robert and Elizabeth Barrett Browning. London, Adam and Charles Black, 1901.
Copy L

E275 : Sonnets . . . London, R. B. Johnson, 1901.
Copy C

E276 : Sonnets from the Portuguese. Edinburgh, O. Schulze and Co., 1901. ,
Copies TxWB L O

E277 : Sonnets from the Portuguese. Preface by Edmund Gosse, Portland, Maine, [Second Edition.] Thomas B. Mosher, 1901.
Copies DLC MH CtY

E278 : Aurora Leigh, and other Poems. London, Henry Frowde, 1902. (The Oxford Miniature Edition).
Copies L O

E279 : Sonnets from the Portuguese. New York, G. P. Putnam's Sons [1902].
Copies DLC MH MB

E280 : Sonnets from the Portuguese. Boston, Small, Maynard and Co., 1902.
Copy CCC

E281 : Sonnets from the Portuguese. London, George Bell and Sons, 1902.
Copy CtY

E282 : Sonnets from the Portuguese. New York, James Pott and Co., 1902.
Copy NCD

E283 : **Complete Works** . . . Edited with introductions and notes by Charlotte Porter and Helen A. Clarke . . . New York, The Riverdale Press, 1903. 6 V.
Copies ViU Wa CU

E284 : **Poems** . . . With an introduction by Alice Meynell. London, Blackie, 1903. (Red Letter Library).
Copies CtY L O

E285 : **Poetical Works** . . . Edited by Augustine Birrell. Smith, Elder, and Co., 1903.
Copy CaOTU

E286 : **Aurora Leigh.** With introduction by Charlotte Porter and Helen A. Clarke. London, George Bell and Sons, 1902. One of the "Life and Light Books."
Copy L

E287 : **Beautiful Thoughts from Robert and Elizabeth Browning.** Arranged by Margaret Shipp. New York, J. Pott and Co., 1902.
Copy IU

E288 : **Letters of Robert Browning and Elizabeth Barrett Barrett.** New York, Harper and Brothers, 1902.
Copy MOSW

E289 : **Love Poems of Elizabeth Barrett Browning,** including the Sonnets from the Portuguese. London and New York, John Lane, 1902. (Lover's Library).
Copies NN DLC L O

E290 : **Poems** . . . With a Critical and Biographical Introduction by Hamilton W. Mabie. New York, P. F. Collier and Son. [1902].
Copies NCD NN AZTES FU

E291 : **The Sleep.** New York, The Stryvelyne Press, 1902.
Copy MWelC

E292 : **I Sonetti Portoghesi di Elisabetta Barrett-Browning.** Studio e versione Italiana di Teresa Venuti de Dominicis. Roma, 1902.
Copies MWelC L TxWB

E293 : **Poetical Works** . . . W. P. Nimmo, 1903.
Listed English Catalogue. *Not seen.*

E294 : **A Selection from Mrs. Browning's Poems.** Edited by Heloise E. Hersey. New York, London, Macmillan and Co., 1903.
Copies DLC NN MH

E295 : Sonnets from the Portuguese. London, Simpkin, Marshall, Hamilton, Kent, 1903.
Copies DLC CLSU O C

E296 : Sonette nach dem Portugiesischen aus dem Englischen übersetzt von Marie Gothein. Verlegt bei Eugen Diederichs, Leipzig, 1903.
Copies NN LC MH

E297 : Les sonnets du Portugais. Traduits en vers français, avec préface, texte anglais . . . par Léon Morel. Paris, Hachette, 1903.
Copies MH L

E298 : Sonnets from the Portuguese. Preface by Edmund Gosse. Portland, Maine, [Third Edition.] Thomas B. Mosher, 1903.
Copies DLC MH CtY

E299 : Selected Poems . . . Edited with an Introduction and Notes by Elizabeth Lee. Boston . . . Ginn and Co. [1904].
Copies MH ViU OClW L O

E300 : Poems. Boston, H. M. Caldwell Co. [1904].
Copies DLC MiU MH CtY

E301 : Sonnets from the Portuguese. New York, Dodge Publishing Co. 1904.
Copies DLC TxWB

E302 : Sonnets from the Portuguese. London, G. Routledge and Sons, ltd.; New York, E. P. Dutton and Co. [1904]. (The Broadway Booklets.)
Copy CtY

E303 : Sonnets. London, Astolat Press, 1904.
Copy L

E304 : Sonnets from the Portuguese. London, Anthony Treherne and Co., ltd., 1904.
Copies MH L

E305 : Aurora Leigh. India Paper Edition. London, H. R. Allenson, 1905.
Copies L O

E306 : Casa Guidi Windows, and other Poems. London, Henry Frowde, 1904. (The Oxford Miniature Edition.)
Copies L O

E307 : Complete Poems . . . London, George Newnes; New York, Scribner's [1904]. 2 V.
Copies CtY L O

E308 : **Florence in the Poetry of the Brownings.** Chicago, A. C. McClurg and Co., 1904.
Copies DLC CtY WU MWelC

E309 : **The Mrs. Browning Birthday Book.** With an Introduction by Chas. W. Vick. London, G. Routledge; New York, E. P. Dutton, 1904.
Copy CtY

E310 : **Poetical Works** . . . London, New York, H. Frowde, 1904. (Oxford Complete Edition).
Copies CtY L O

E311 : **Poems** . . . With an introduction by Alice Meynell. Boston, New York [1904]. (Red Letter Library).
Copy CtY

E312 : **Poetical Works** . . . London, Smith, Elder, and Co. 1904.
Copy DU

E313 : **Sonnets from the Portuguese.** London, Glasgow, Gowans and Gray, 1905. (Cadogan Booklets No. 1).
Copies L O

E314 : **Elizabeth Barrett Browning in her Letters.** Edited by Percy Lubbock. London, Smith, Elder, and Co., 1906.
Copy OCl (Cited National Union Catalogue. *Not seen*).

E315 : **Lady Geraldine's Courtship.** London, T. C. and E. C. Jack; New York, E. P. Dutton and Co. [1906].
Copies MB L O

E316 : **Love Sonnets** . . . A Selection. Edinburgh and London. T. N. Foulis [1906]. (Roses of Parnassus No. 15).
Copy L

E317 : **Poetical Works** . . . London, H. Frowde, 1906. (Oxford Complete Edition).
Copies MiU OClW NN L

E318 : **Poetical Works** . . . London, Smith, Elder, and Co., 1906.
Copy MiDW

E319 : **Aurora Leigh.** London, Maclaren and Co., [1905?].
Copy C

E320 : **Poetical Works** . . . New York, The Macmillan Co., 1905.
Copies DCU NNC OCU

E321 : **Poetical Works** . . . Chicago, The Henneberry Co. [1905].
Copy IU

E322 : The Religious Opinions of Elizabeth Barrett Browning. London, Hodder and Stoughton, 1906.
Copy MH

E323 : Les Sonnets Portugais . . . traduits en sonnets français, avec notice, texte anglais, commentaire et notes par Fernand Henry. Paris, E. Guilmoto, 1905.
Copies MWelC DLC L

E324 : Sonnets from the Portuguese. New York, Grosset and Dunlap [1905?].
Copy PPIU (Not seen).

E325 : Sonnets from the Portuguese and other Poems . . . One word more and other Poems. With an introduction by Richard Watson Gilder. New York, The Century Co., 1905.
Copies DLC ViU MB L

E326 : The Religious Opinions of Elizabeth Barrett Browning. London, Hodder & Stoughton, 1906.
Copies MH L

E327 : Sonnets from the Portuguese. Philadelphia, George W. Jacobs and Co. [1906].
Copies CSt MH

E328 : Sonnets from the Portuguese. Chiswick, London, The Caradoc Press, 1906.
Copies NN TxWB Le

E329 : Sonnets from the Portuguese. London, Chapman and Hall [1906].
Copy L

E330 : Sonnets from the Portuguese. Preface by Edmund Gosse [Fourth Edition] Portland, Maine, T. B. Mosher, 1906.
Copies MH ViU IU

E331 : Sonnets from the Portuguese. Venice, S. Rosen, 1906.
Copies MWelC ViU TxU CSmH

E332 : Beautiful Thoughts from Robert and Elizabeth Browning. New York, J. Pott and Co., 1907.
Copy NCU

E333 : Florence in the Poetry of the Brownings. Second Edition. Chicago, A. C. McClurg and Co., 1907.
Copies NHD MOU ORU

E334 : **Lady Geraldine's Courtship.** New York, D. Appleton and Co., 1907.
Copies DLC CtY L O

E335 : **Poetical Works** . . . London, Smith, Elder, and Co., 1907.
Copy WaSpG

E336 : **Rhyme of the Duchess May.** London and Edinburgh. T. N. Foulis [1907].
Copies DLC MiU CtY L O

E337 : **Select Poems by Robert Browning and Elizabeth Barrett Browning.** With Introduction and Notes by Emma F. Lowd and Mary C. Craig. New York, Boston . . . University Publishing Co., 1907.
Copies DLC NNC RPB

E338 : **The Sleep** . . . London, A. Fairbairns and Co., 1907.
Copies L O

E339 : **I Sonetti Portoghesi,** Studio e Versione Italiana de Teresa Venuti de Dominicis, Verona, 1907.
Copy TxWB

E340 : **Sonnets from the Portuguese.** London, T. C. and E. C. Jack [1907].
Copies L O

E341 : **The Cry of the Children.** [New York, 1908]. (Child Labor Committee Pamphlets No. 66).
Copy NN

E342 : **Poetical Works** . . . London and Glasgow, Collins [1908–09]. 2 V.
Copy CU

E343 : **Rhyme of the Duchess May.** Philadelphia, G. W. Jacobs and Co. [1908].
Copy MH

E344 : **Sonnette nach dem Portugiesischen.** Übertragen durch Rainer Maria Rilke. Leipzig, Insel-verlag 1908 ⟨first edition⟩
Copies CtY DLC NjP MH L

E345 : **Sonnets from the Portuguese.** London, Siegle, Hill, and Co., 1908. (Langham Booklets).
Copy L

E346 : **Sonnets from the Portuguese.** London, George Bell and Sons, 1908.
Copies DLC MH

E347 : **Casa Guidi Windows.** With an introduction by Mary F. Robinson. London, John Lane, 1909.
Copy OO

E348 : **Lady Geraldine's Courtship.** Philadelphia, H. Altemus Co., 1909.
Copy DLC

E349 : **Love Poems from the Works of Robert Browning and Elizabeth Barrett Browning.** Selected and Arranged by Ethel Harris. Chicago, New York, Rand McNally and Co. [c 1909].
Copy DLC

E350 : **Die Sonette aus dem Portugiesischen und andere Gedichte,** in Deutscher Übertragung von Helene Scheu-Reisz. Axel Juncker Verlag, Berlin-Charlottenburg [1909].
Copies MH DLC

E351 : **Sonnets from the Portuguese.** [Fifth Edition.] Portland, Maine, Thomas B. Mosher, 1909.
Copy ORU

E352 : **Sonnets . . .** London, Siegle, Hill, and Co., 1909.
Copy TxWB

E353 : **Sonnets from the Portuguese.** New York, Duffield and Co., 1909.
Copies MH DLC

E354 : **Poetical Works . . .** London, New York, H. Frowde, 1910. (Oxford Edition).
Copies DLC NCC

E355 : **The Romaunt of the Page.** London and Glasgow, Collins [c 1910].
Copy L

E356 : **Sonnets from the Portuguese.** New York, G. P. Putnam's Sons [1910]. (Ariel Booklets).
Copies PU CDU IEN

E357 : **Sonnets from the Portuguese.** New York, Barse and Hopkins [c 1910]. (The Golden Books).
Copies MH PU PP L

E358 : **Sonnets.** London, Siegle, Hill, and Co., 1910. (Queen's Library of Literary Treasures).
Copies O L

E359 : Sonnets from the Portuguese. Preface by Edmund Gosse. Portland, Maine, [Sixth Edition.] T. B. Mosher, 1910.
Copies ViU MH

E360 : Sonnets from the Portuguese, with Lyric Interludes . . . Edited with Preface, Notes, and Appendix Introducing Robert Browning's Related Poems, by Arthur Guiterman. San Francisco, Paul Elder, and Co. [c 1910].
Copies PBL MB DLC CLU-C

E361 : Sonnets from the Portuguese. London, Henry Frowde [1909]. (Moment Series).
Copy L

E362 : Sonnets from the Portuguese. London, John Ouseley [1909].
Copy L

E363 : Sonnets from the Portuguese. Introduction by Alice Meynell. London, T. Fisher Unwin, ltd., [1909].
Copies CLU-C OCl PBL

E364 : Sonnets from the Portuguese, and Other Sonnets. London, Samuel Bagster and Sons, [1909].
Copies L TxWB

E365 : Entry Cancelled.

E366 : The Letters of Elizabeth Barrett Browning. Edited with Biographical Additions by F. G. Kenyon . . . New York, The Macmillan Co.; London, Macmillan and Co., ltd., 1910.
Copies OCLW ODW CtY

E367 : Poems.Domes of Silence, 1910.
Listed English Catalogue. *Not seen.*

E368 : Entry cancelled.

E369 : From Day to Day with the Brownings. Compiled by Wallace and Frances Rice. New York, Barse and Hopkins [c 1911].
Copy DLC

E370 : Lady Geraldine's Courtship. London, Siegle, Hill, and Co. [1911]. (Langham Booklets).
Copy L

E371 : Love Sonnets . . . London, A. L. Humphreys, 1911.
Copies L O

E372 : Love Sonnets. Siegle, Hill, 1911.
Listed English Catalogue. *Not seen.*

E373 : My Kate. London, Henry Frowde, and Hodder & Stoughton [1911].
Copy L

E374 : Poetical Works . . . London, Henry Frowde, 1911.
Copy TxWB

E375 : Portugiesische Sonette. In Deutsche Blankverse. Übertragen von Hans Böhm. Munich, Callwey, 1911.
Copy NJP

E376 : Selections from E. B. Browning. Siegle, Hill, 1911.
Listed English Catalogue. *Not seen.*

E377 : Sonette aus dem Portugiesischen. Übertragen durch Rainer Maria Rilke. Zweite Auflage. Leipzig, 1911.
Copies CtY MH

E378 : Sonnets from the Portuguese. London, Hodder and Stoughton [1911].
Copies L O

E379 : Sonnets from the Portuguese. London, Arthur L. Humphreys, 1911.
Copy DT

E380 : Poems . . . London, Oxford University Press, 1912. (World's Classics).
Copies L O

E381 : Poetical Works. W. P. Nimmo, 1912.
Listed English Catalogue. *Not seen.*

E382 : Poetical Works . . . Philadelphia, J. C. Winston Co. [1912?].
Copies MH NNU

E383 : Sonnets from the Portuguese. London, St. Catherine Press [1912] (Arden Books No. 2).
Copies L O

E384 : Sonnets from the Portuguese, and Other Poems. Edinburgh, W. P. Nimmo and Co., 1912.
Copies OC L O

E385 : Sonnets from the Portuguese. Siegle, Hill, 1912.
Listed English Catalogue of Books. *Not seen.*

E386 : Through the Year with Mrs. Browning . . . Boston, Dewolfe, Fiske, and Co. [1912?].
Copies IU MH CtY

E387 : **Thoughts from Mrs. Browning.** Selections from the Writings . . . for Every Day in the Year. Edited by Ann Bachelor. Boston, J. H. Earle [c 1912].
Copy CtY

E388 : **Analecta from Mrs. Browning's Letters,** Gathered by Mary Trammell Scott. New York, The Bookery Publishing Co., 1913.
Copy TxWB

E389 : **Poetical Works** . . . London, Humphrey Milford, 1913. (Oxford Edition).
Copies NN NCM Liv

E390 : **Sonnets from the Portuguese.** London, Arthur L. Humphreys, 1913.
Copy TxWB

E391 : **Sonnets from the Portuguese.** Portland, Maine, T. B. Mosher, 1913.
Copy CtY

E392 : **Sonnets from the Portuguese.** Rome, 1913.
Copy DLC (photocopy)

E393 : **Sonnets.** Siegle, Hill, 1913.
Listed English Catalogue. *Not seen.*

E394 : **An E. B. Browning Birthday Book.** London, Siegle, Hill, and Co. [1914]. (Langham Birthday Books).
Copy L

E395 : **Complete Poetical Works** . . . With a Prefatory Note by Robert Browning. New York, Thomas Y. Crowell Co. [1914?]
Copy ViU

E396 : **An Epistle to a Canary.** Preface by Edmund Gosse. New York, The Macmillan Co., 1914.
Copies DLC MB CtY

E397 : **Poems,** Selected. Frowde, 1913. (World's Classics).
Listed English Catalogue. *Not seen.*

E398 : **Poetical Works** . . . London, John Murray, 1914.
Copy C–VicPR

E399 : **Selections from Robert and Elizabeth Barrett Browning.**
Siegle, Hill, 1914.
Listed English Catalogue. *Not seen.*

E400 : Sonnets from the Portuguese. [London, Published for the Medici Society by P. L. Warner, [1914]. (The Riccardi Press Booklets).
Copies CSt TxU L O

E401 : A True Dream. New York, The Macmillan Co., 1914.
Copy DLC

E402 : New Poems . . . Edited by Sir Frederic G. Kenyon. New York, The Macmillan Co., 1915.
Copies TxWB TxU DLC MWelC

E403 : Poetical Works; with Two Prose Essays. London, Humphrey Milford, 1916. (Oxford Edition).
Copies NN MB

E404 : Sonnets from the Portuguese. New York, Dodge Publishing Co., 1916.
Copies TxWB OFH O

E405 : Elizabeth Barrett Browning in her Letters. Edited by Percy Lubbock. London, John Murray, 1917.
Copies ICarbS PST

E406 : Sonnets from the Portuguese. East Aurora, New York, the Roycroft Shop [c 1917].
Copy DLC

E407 : I Sonetti dal Portoghese. Trad. C. Chiarini. [Spezia "Arti Grafiche"] 1917.
Copy IEN

E408 : Complete Poetical Works . . . With an Introduction by Lilian Whiting. New York, Thomas Nelson and Sons, 1918. 2 V.
Copy MB

E409 : Poetical Works . . . With an introduction by Alice Meynell. London, Ward, Lock, and Co. [1918?].
Copy MCHB

E410 : Drei portugiesische Sonette nach Übertragen von Rainer Maria Rilke vertont von Erich Anders. Berlin, Carl Hermann [1918].
Copy MH

E411 : Sonetti dal Portoghese. Trad. C. Chiarini, Milano, 1918.
Copy TxWB

E412 : Sonnets from the Portuguese. St. Catherine, 1918. (The Arden Books).
Listed English Catalogue. *Not seen.*

E413 : **Complete Poetical Works** ... With an Introduction by Lilian Whiting. New York, Thomas Nelson and Sons [1919]. 2 V. (New Century Library).
Copy L

E414 : **Sonette aus dem Portugiesischen.** Übertragen durch Rainer Maria Rilke. Im Insel-Verlag zu Leipzig [1919].
Copies MH CtY ICU

E415 : **Sonnets from the Portuguese.** Harrap, 1919.
Listed English Catalogue. *Not seen.*

E416 : **Sonnets from the Portuguese.** New York, Thomas Y. Crowell Co. [191-].
Copies DLC OCl MH

E417 : **Sonnets from the Portuguese.** New York and London, G. P. Putnam's Sons [191-].
Copy CtY

E418 : **Sonnets from the Portuguese.** New York, Platt and Peck Co. [191-].
Copy MH

E419 : **Poetical Works** ... London, Oxford ... Oxford University Press, 1920.
Copies MH PP NNU

E420 : **Die Sonette aus dem Portugiesischen.** In deutscher Übertragung von Helen Scheu-Riesz. 2 Aufl. Berlin, Juncker [1920].
Copy MH

E421 : **Sonette aus dem Portugiesischen.** Nachdictung von Hans Wolfgang von Herwarth. München, Mussarion Verlag, 1920.
Copies MH DLC L

E422 : **Sonnets from the Portuguese.** New York, Dodge Publishing Co. [1920].
Copy L

E423 : **Die Sonette aus dem Portugiesischen und andere Gedichte** in deutscher Übertragung von Helen Scheu-Riesz. 2 Aufl. Berlin, A. Juncker [1921].
Copies MH L

E424 : **Selections** ... L. B. Hill, 1922.
Listed English Catalogue. *Not seen.*

E425 : **Sonnets from the Portuguese.** Bath [England], C. Bayntun, 1922.
Copies LU NSyU

E426 : Poems . . . With an introduction by Alice Meynell. London and Glasgow, Blackie and Son [1923].
Copy DLC

E427 : Letters of Robert Browning and Elizabeth Barrett Barrett. London, John Murray [1923]. 2 V. in 1.
Copy INND

E428 : Sonnets from the Portuguese. New York, Dodge Publishing Co. [c 1923].
Copies ORU TxWB

E429 : A Musical Instrument. New Preston, Conn., Bernhardt Wall, 1924.
Copy TxWB

E430 : Sonnets from the Portuguese. London, T. Fisher Unwin, [1924].
Copy L

E431 : Sonety . . . Z. Angielskiego Przelozyla, Z. Reutt-Witkowska, Warszawa, 1924. Instytut Wydawniczy, Bibljoteka, Polska.
Copy TxWB

E432 : Poetical Works. Collins, 1925.
Listed English Catalogue. *Not seen.*

E433 : Sonnets from the Portuguese. [Montagnola, Officina Bodoni, 1925].
Copies NN TxWB NJP NHD

E434 : Sonnets from the Portuguese. With an introduction by Aurelia Henry Reinhardt. San Francisco, J. H. Nash, 1925.
Copies MH ViU CLU–C TxWB

E435 : Casa Guidi Windows, with a prefatory note by William A. Sim. Florentine Illustrated edition. Florence, [Giannini], 1926.
Copies DLC OrP CST TxWB

E436 : The Letters of Robert Browning and Elizabeth Barrett Barrett 1845–1846. New York and London, Harper and Brothers [c 1926]. 2 V.
Copy CtY

E437 : Sonnets from the Portuguese. With Some Observations and a Bibliographical Note by William Andrews Clark, Jr. With Facsimile Reprint of the 1847 Edition. San Francisco, J. H. Nash, 1927.
Copies TxU NN MB DLC L

E437.1 : **Sonette aus dem Portugiesischen.** Übertragen durch Rainer Maria Rilke. Leipzig, Insel-Verlag, 1927.
Copy L

E438 : **Lady Geraldine's Courtship and Sonnets from the Portuguese.** Little Blue Book Company, 1928.
Listed English Catalogue. *Not seen.*

E439 : **Poems.** Collins, 1928.
Listed English Catalogue. *Not seen.*

E440 : **Sonnets from the Portuguese.** [East Aurora, N. Y., Roycroft Shop, 1928].
Copy MB

E441 : **Sonnets from the Portuguese.** New York, Outing Publishing Co. [1928]. (The Golden Books).
Copies ICarbS MWelC OC

E442 : **Sonnets from the Portuguese.** Florence, Giannini, [1929]. (Florentine Edition).
Copies PP OrP

E443 : **Poems** . . . With an introduction by Alice Meynell. London, The Gresham Publishing Co. [192–].
Copies IU MCHB

E444 : **Elizabeth Barrett Browning: Letters to her Sister, 1846–1859.** Edited by Leonard Huxley. New York, E. P. Dutton and Co. [1930].
Copies PP NIC MiU TxWB

E445 : **EBB** . . . **Letters to her Sister.** London, John Murray, 1931.
Copies ICU GEU

E446 : **Sonette aus dem Portugiesischen.** Übertragen durch Rainer Maria Rilke. Leipzig, Insel-verlag [1931].
Copies MH L

E447 : **Sonnets from the Portuguese.** Andrew Vargish [Boston] 1931.
Copy MB

E448 : **Poetical Works** . . . London, Oxford University Press. Humphrey Milford, 1932.
Copies DLC MH CtY

E448.1 : **A Letter to Napoleon III in Behalf of Victor Hugo.** Privately Printed for George Arents, Jr. New York, 1932.
Copies CtY MH NN

E449 : Sonnets from the Portuguese. London, New York, Harper and Brothers, [1932].
Copies CtY DLC NN

E450 : Sonnets from the Portuguese. Oxford, Printed at the Shakespeare Head Press, published by B. Blackwell, 1933. (The Shakespeare Head Quartos, No. 6).
Copies IU OCI L

E451 : Sonnets from the Portuguese. With introduction and notes by Charlotte and Helen A. Clarke. New York, Thomas Y. Crowell Co. [1933].
Copies NIC CT NLC CtY

E452 : Two Poets, a Dog, and a Boy, Being a Selection of Verse from Robert and Elizabeth Barrett Browning . . . [compiled] by Frances Theresa Russell. Philadelphia and London, J. B. Lippincott Co. [1933].
Copies DLC NIC MH

E453 : The Letters of Robert Browning and Elizabeth Barrett Barrett. London, John Murray [1934] 2 V. in 1.
Copy MCHB

E454 : Sonnets de la Portugaise . . . traduction d'Emile B. D'Erlanger. Londres, Burrup, Mathieson and Co. [1935].
Copies DLC L

E455 : Sonnets from the Portuguese. Mount Vernon, [New York] Peter Pauper Press [1935].
Copies NN NPV

E456 : . . . Portugal szonettek. Máté József Fordítása. Budapest, Pantheon-Kiadas, 1936.
Copy NN

E457 : Sonnets from the Portuguese. With introduction by Charlotte Porter and Helen A. Clarke. New York, Thomas Y. Crowell [c 1936].
Copies DLC TxU PP CtY

E458 : Sonnets from the Portuguese. London, R. Riviere and Son, 1936.
Copy L

E459 : Sonnets from the Portuguese. [New York] Concord Books [1937].
Copies NNC MH

E460 : Sonnets from the Portuguese. New York, Hartsdale House [1937].
Copies NC GW NHD

E461 : Sonnets from the Portuguese. New York, Illustrated Editions Co. [c 1937].
Copies CU CST TxWB

E462 : Sonnets from the Portuguese. Mount Vernon, [New York], Peter Pauper Press, 1937.
Copies NN DeU

E463 : Sonnets from the Portuguese. New York, Three Sirens Press [c 1937].
Copy DLC

E464 : Sonnets from the Portuguese. New York, For the Members of the Heritage Club [c 1938].
Copies DLC NN MH MB

E465 : Sonnets from the Portuguese. New York, Grosset and Dunlap [1938?].
Copy KAstB

E466 : Sonnets from the Portuguese. Oxford, Shakespeare Head Press, 1938. (Shakespeare Head Quartos).
Copy NN

E467 : Sonnets from the Portuguese. Mount Vernon, [New York], Peter Pauper Press, [1938].
Copy OCl

E468 : Sonnets de la Portugaise. Traduits de L'Anglais par Le Baron Emile B. D'Erlanger, Paris, Librairie Istra [1938].
Copies TxWB L

E469 : Sonnets from the Portuguese. [Cambridge, England], Rampant Lions Press [1939].
Copies ICN PSC NN

E470 : Sonnets from the Portuguese. Second Edition. Oxford, Shakespeare Head Press, 1939.
Copies ICarbS DT

E471 : Portugeesche sonnetten, vrij bewerkt naar het Engelsch door Helene Swarth. [Amsterdam, Maatschappij voor Goede en Goedkoope Lectuur, 193-].
Copies DLC MH

E472 : **Un poema de Amor; Sonetos del portugueses** ... Interpretu-dos en prosa por Lola Tosi de Dieguez y en verso por Ana Luisa Machline. Buenos Aires [Geronimo J. Pesco, 1940].
Copy DPU

E473 : **Sonette aus dem Portugiesischen.** Übertragen durch Rainer Maria Rilke. Leipzig, Insel-Verlag, 1941.
Copy MH

E474 : **The Best Known Poems of Elizabeth and Robert Brown-ing.** Garden City, New York, Halcyon House [1942]. (Blue Rib-bon Books).
Copies MB NCU ORU

E475 : **Sonnets from the Portuguese.** New York, Holiday House [1942].
Copy MH

E476 : **Sonetos del Portugues.** Traduccion y nota de Ernestina de Champourcin. Mexico, Rueca [1942].
Copies TxU IU

E477 : **Stanzas, a fragment.** March, 1845 [by] Elizabeth Barrett Browning. Stanford University. Nathan van Patten, 1942.
Copies CSt Cty

E478 : **Stanzas, a fragment,** March, 1845 [by] Elizabeth Barrett Browning. Stanford University Library, 1943.
Copies DLC NN TxWB

E479 : **Sonnets from the Portuguese,** avec une traduction en vers français et une introduction par André Maurois. [New York]. Bren-tano's [1944].
Copies MB DLC CU

E480 : **Sonnets from the Portuguese.** New York, The Heritage Re-prints [1945].
Copy MB

E481 : **Sonnets from the Portuguese.** Introduction and notes by Charlotte E. Porter and Helen A. Clarke. New York, Thomas Y. Crowell Co. [1945].
Copies DLC CU

E482 : **Sonnets** ... Traduits par Alliette Audra. Paris, 1945.
Copy L

E483 : **Love poems of Elizabeth Barrett Browning and Robert Browning;** Selected and with a Forward by Louis Untermeyer. New Brunswick, N.J., Rutgers University Press [1946].
Copies DLC MH IU

E484 : **Sonnets from the Portuguese.** With Introductions and Notes by Charlotte E. Porter and Helen A. Clarke. New York, Thomas Y. Crowell Co. [1946]. (Half Hour Classics).
Copies ViU TxWB

E485 : **Sonnets from the Portuguese.** Edited by Adrian S. Mott. Oxford, B. Blackwell, 1946. (Shakespeare Head Quartos no. 6).
Copy L

E486 : **The Poetry of the Brownings.** An Anthology Compiled by Clifford Bax. London, F. Muller [1947].
Copies MH CU CLU-C DLC L

E487 : **Sonnets from the Portuguese.** With an Introduction by A. S. Mott. Oxford, Shakespeare Head Press, 1947.
Copy LU

E488 : **Poems.** With an Introduction by Samuel J. Looker. London, Grey Walls Press [1948].
Copies MH CtY L

E489 : **Sonnets from the Portuguese.** New York, Heritage Press [c 1948].
Copies CU INND RPB

E490 : **Sonnets from the Portuguese.** With an Introduction by Louis Untermeyer. For members of the Limited Editions Club, New York, 1948.
Copies MB MH DLC

E491 : **Sonnets from the Portuguese.** New York, Grossett and Dunlap [194–]. (Cameo Classics).
Copies GEU MOSW TxWB

E492 : **Sonnets from the Portuguese.** Philadelphia, David McKay [194–]. (Pocket Classics).
Copies NN TxWB PU NCC

E493 : **Sonnets from the Portuguese.** Mount Vernon, N.Y. Golden Eagle Press [194–].
Copies NN NCGW TxWB

E494 : **Sonnets from the Portuguese.** Mt. Vernon, New York, Peter Pauper Press [194–].
Copies ViU PU MSU

E495 : **The Best Known Poems of Elizabeth and Robert Browning.** Garden City, N.Y., Doubleday [1950?].
Copy ViU

E496 : **Prometheus Bound** . . . With an Introduction by Walter R. Agard. New York, The Liberal Arts Press [1950].
Copies NCD PST NNC

E497 : **Sonnets from the Portuguese.** New York, Avon Publishing Co. [c 1950]. (Avon Classics).
Copy MWelC

E498 : **Sonnets from the Portuguese.** New York, Thomas Y. Crowell Co. [1950].
Copies DLC NlC TxWB

E499 : **Sonnets from the Portuguese.** Centennial Variorum Edition. With an Introduction by Fannie Ratchford. New York, P. C. Duschnes, 1950.
Copies MH DLC TxU L

E500 : **Sonnets from the Portuguese.** Garden City, New York, Halcyon House [1950?].
Copy DLC

E501 : **Sonnets from the Portuguese.** Chicago, Henry Regnery, [1950].
Copies MWelC IU TxWB

E502 : **Love's Alchemy; Selections from Sonnets from the Portuguese.** Waco, Texas, Sigma Tau Delta, Baylor University, 1951.
Copies TxWB NNC

E503 : **Poetical Works** . . . London, Oxford University Press, Geoffrey Cumberlege, 1951.
Copy DCP

E504 : **Sonnets from the Portuguese.** Mount Vernon, New York, Peter Pauper Press. [1951].
Copy NNC

E505 : **Prometheus Bound** . . . Ithaca, New York, Abbe Press [1952].
Copies DLC NCD NNC INND

E506 : **Sonette aus dem Portugiesischen.** Übertragen durch Rainer Maria Rilke. [Leipzig] Insel-Verlag [1952].
Copy SCU

E507 : **Sonnets from the Portuguese.** New York, Heritage Press, [1952].
Copy OU (Cited National Union Catalogue. *Not seen.*)

E508 : **Sonnets from the Portuguese, and Other Love Poems.** Garden City, New York, Hanover House [1954]. Copies MH OCL CEac

E509 : **Sonetos del portugués.** Versión y prologo de Julieta Gomez Paz. Madrid, Rialp, 1954. Copies IU MH CU

E510 : **Sonnets from the Portuguese.** Translated into Russian by Michael Zetlin and Igor Astrow, Foreword by George Adamovich, [Experiments] New York, 1956. Copies MH DLC IEN

E511 : . . . **Sonnets from the Portugese.** Préf de Ronald Armstrong. Monaco, Editions du Rocher [1957]. Copy IU

E512 : **Sonnets from the Portuguese and Seven Other Poems.** Utrecht, De Roos, 1957. Copy CLU-C

E513 : **Sonnets from the Portuguese.** Traduction de M. Bottinelli-Jérome. Lausanne, Bottinelli [1958]. Copy MH

E514 : **Sonnets from the Portuguese.** Chicago, The Printing Office of Philip Reed [1951?]. Copy KYU

E515 : **Sonnets from the Portuguese.** Westwood, New Jersey, Revell [1961]. Copies MH DLC

E516 : **Sonnets from the Portuguese.** Introduction by Dorothy Hewlett. London, Folio Society, 1962. Copies NN MH CoU

E517 : **Sonnets from the Portuguese, and Other Poems.** Garden City, New York, Doubleday Co. [1962?]. A Dolphin Book, C 209. Copies OCl TxWB

UNDATED EDITIONS

E518 : **Aurora Leigh.** New York, Dodd, Mead, and Co., [n.d.]. Copies MH PPL OCL

E519 : **Aurora Leigh.** New York, Dodd, Mead, and Co. [n.d.]. Copies MH C-Vu

E520 : **Aurora Leigh.** Chicago, Belford, Clarke [n.d.].
Copies UU IdU TxWB

E521 : **Poems and Sonnets from the Portuguese.** With a Biographical and Critical Sketch by D. S. Douglas . . . New York, R. M. McBride & Co. [n.d.].
Copy FU (Cited National Union Catalogue. *Not seen*).

E522 : **Elizabeth Barrett Browning** [Poems] . . . Chicago, M. A. Donohue Co. [n.d.].
Copy TxWB

E523 : **Lady Geraldine's Courtship.** London, Review of Reviews [n.d.]. (The Penny Poets).
Copy OO

E524 : **Sonette aus dem Portugiesischen;** nachdichtung von Hans-Wolfgang von Herwarth. [n.p.] [n.d.].
Copy ODW

E525 : **Sonnets from the Portuguese.** Girard, Kansas, Haldeman-Julius Co., [n.d.].
Copy ViU

E526 : **Sonnets from the Portuguese.** London, Selfridge and Co., Ltd, [n.d.]
Copy TxWB

E527 : **Sonnets from the Portuguese.** Jamaica, Edmund S. Wood, [n.d.].
Copy TxWB

E528 : **Sonetos Portugueses.** Traducos de Manuel Correa de Barros, Livraria Figuerinhas, Porto [n.d.].
Copy TxWB

E529 : **Sonnets from the Portuguese.** New York, Little Leather Library Corporation. [n.d.]
Copy TxWB

INDEX OF TEXTUAL VARIANTS

"See that rock which o'er looks the turbulent deep" B9

Sent to Mama on 1st May, 1814 B9

Seraph and Poet, The c52 †A5 A6 A8 A10

Seraphim, The A4 †A6 †A8 A10

Ship Being Lost at Tynemouth, On a B9

Sleep, The A4 †A6 A8 A10

Sleeping and Watching †A5 †A6 A8 A10 = The Child and the Watcher c54

"Soft as the dew from Heaven descends" B9

"Soft were the murmurs of the gentle rill" B9

Song, A [Is't loving to list to the night guitar] B4 B9

Song [I stood by the river where twain of us stood] B9 = That Day †A5 †A6 A8 A10

Song, A [Peter Quarry he called all his vices together] B9

Song [Weep, as if you thought of laughter!] A2

Song Against Singing, A A4 †A6 A8 A10

Song for the Ragged Schools of London, A9 = A Plea for the Ragged Schools of London †A13

Sonnet, A Sketch c60 = Two Sketches II †A6 †A8 A10

Sonnet on Mr. Haydon's Portrait of Mr. Wordsworth c37 = On a Portrait of Wordsworth by B. R. Haydon †A5 A6 A8 A10

Sonnets from the Portuguese

⟨1⟩ "I thought once how Theocritus had sung" A6 A8 A10

⟨2⟩ "But only three in all God's Universe" A6 A8 A10

⟨3⟩ "Unlike are we, unlike, O princely Heart!" A6 A8 A10

⟨4⟩ "Thou hast thy calling to some palace floor" A6 A8 A10

⟨5⟩ "I lift my heavy heart up solemnly" A6 A8 A10

⟨6⟩ "Go from me. Yet I feel that I shall stand" A6 A8 A10

⟨7⟩ "The face of all the world is changed, I think" A6 A8 A10

⟨8⟩ "What can I give thee back, O liberal" A6 A8 A10

⟨9⟩ "Can it be right to give what I can give?" A6 A8 A10

⟨10⟩ "Yet, love, mere love is beautiful indeed" A6 A8 A10

⟨11⟩ "And therefore if to love can be desert" A6 A8 †A10

⟨12⟩ "Indeed this very love which is my boast" A6 A8 †A10

⟨13⟩ "And wilt thou have me fashion into speech" A6 A8 A10

⟨14⟩ "If thou must love me, let it be for nought" A6 A8 †A10

⟨15⟩ "Accuse me not, beseech thee, that I wear" A6 A8 A10

⟨16⟩ "And yet, because thou overcomest so" A6 A8 †A10

⟨17⟩ "My poet, thou canst touch on all the notes" A6 A8 A10

⟨18⟩ "I never gave a lock of hair away"A6 A8 A10

⟨19⟩ "The soul's Rialto hath its merchandise;" A6 A8 A10

⟨20⟩ "Beloved, my Beloved, when I think" A6 A8 A10

⟨21⟩ "Say over again and yet once over again" A6 A8 A10

⟨22⟩ "When our two souls stand up erect and strong" A6 A8 A10

⟨23⟩ "Is it indeed so? If I lay here dead" A6 A8 A10

⟨24⟩ "Let the world's sharpness, like a clasping knife." A6 A8 A10

⟨25⟩ "A heavy heart, Beloved, have I borne" A6 A8 A10

⟨26⟩ "I lived with visions for my company" A6 A8 A10

⟨27⟩ "My own Beloved, who hast lifted me" A6 A8 A10

⟨28⟩ "My letters! all dead paper, mute and white!" A6 A8 A10

⟨29⟩ "I think of thee!—my thoughts do twine and bud" A6 A8 A10

⟨30⟩ "I see thine image through my tears tonight" A6 A8 A10

⟨31⟩ "Thou comest! all is said without a word." A6 A8 A10

⟨32⟩ "The first time that the sun rose on thine oath" A6 A8 A10

⟨33⟩ "Yes, call me by my pet-name! let me hear" A6 A8 A10

⟨34⟩ "With the same heart, I said, I'll answer thee" A6 A8 A10

⟨35⟩ "If I leave all for thee, wilt thou exchange" A6 A8 A10

⟨36⟩ "When we met first and loved, I did not build" A6 A8 A10

⟨37⟩ "Pardon, oh, pardon, that my soul should make" A6 A8 †A10

⟨38⟩ "First time he kissed me, he but only kissed" A6 A8 A10

⟨39⟩ "Because thou hast the power and own'st the grace" A6 †A8 A10

⟨40⟩ "Oh, yes! they love through all this world of ours!" A6 A8 A10

⟨41⟩ "I thank all who have loved me in their hearts" A6 A8 †A10

⟨42⟩ " '*My future will not copy fair my past*' " A10 = Future and Past A5 A6 A8

⟨42⟩ "How do I love thee? Let me count the ways" A6 A8 = ⟨43⟩ A10

⟨43⟩ "Beloved, thou has brought me many flowers" A6 A8 = ⟨44⟩ A10

PROSE

Queen Annelida and False Arcite C30
Song of the Rose [Attributed to Sappho] A13
Soyez satisfaite, O génération d'Adam B9
Translation from Claudian B6 B9
Translation from Dante, Inferno B9
Translation of the Ninth Satire of Horace's first Book B9
Translation from Plato, Dialogue between Criton and Socrates B9

DRAMA

Princess Caroline of Brunswick and Her Daughter B9
Prologue B9
Regulus B9

INDEX OF TITLES

INDEX OF PRINTERS, PUBLISHERS, EDITORS, TRANSLATORS

Rinder, E. W. E242
Riverdale Press, The E283
Riviere, R. and Son E458
Robinson, A. M. F. E273
Robinson, Mary F. E347
Rolfe, W. J. E158
Rosen, S. E331
Routledge, George and Sons E170 E171 E217 E249 E302 E309
Roycroft Shop, The E240 E406 E440
Rueca E476
Russell, Frances Theresa E452
Rutgers University Press E483

St. Catherine Press E383 E412
Saunders and Otley A4
Scheu-Riesz, Helene E350 E420 E423
Schulze, O. and Co. E276
Scott, Mary Trammell E388
Scott, Walter, Ltd. E242
Scribner, Charles and Co. E59 E62 E307
Selfridge and Co., Ltd. E526
Seymour, R. F. E250
Shakespeare Head Press E450 E466 E470 E487
Shackford, M. H. D24
Shipp, Margaret E257 E287
Shorter, Clement D15
Siegle, Hill and Co. E352 E358 E345 E370 E372 E376 E385 E393
E394 E399
Sigma Tau Delta, Baylor University E502
Sim, William A. E435
Simpkin, Marshall, Hamilton, Kent E206 E295
Small, Maynard and Co. E280
Smith, Elder, and Co. B10 D13 D14 E60.1 E61 E64 E69 E73 E80
E87 E95 E104 E109 E114 E120 E123 E124 E125 E126 E128 E135
E136 E138 E140 E145 E151 E156 E159 E160 E161 E162 E169
E182 E186.1 E190 E196 E200 E207 E216 E221 E223 E231 E233
E255 E260 E285 E312 E314 E318 E335
Society of English and French Literature E64
Spottiswood and Co., Ltd. B10
Sproul, George D. E274
Stanford University E477
Stanford University Library E478
Stoddard, R. H. E131 E185 E192 E198
Stokes, Frederick A. Co. E197 E202 E214
Stone, James H. E23
Stryvelyne Press, The E291
Swarth, Helene E471
Swinburne, Algernon Charles E231 E255
Syndicate Trading Co. E108

Tauchnitz, B. E76 E81
Taylor, John Edward A13 A14
Three Sirens Press E463
Ticknor and Co. E157 E177
Ticknor and Fields E40
Tilton, Theodore E26 E32 E37 E47
Traquair, Phoebe Ann E228
Treherne, Anthony and Co., Ltd. E304
Tuckerman, Henry T. E3 E7 E8 E9 E28 E60 E180 E214

United Feature Syndicate, The D22
Universal Publishing Co. E183
University of Illinois Press D36
University Publishing Co. E337
Untermeyer, Louis E483 E490
Unwin, T. Fisher, Ltd. E363 E430

Vale Press E229
Valpy, A. J. A3
vanPatten, Nathan E477
Vargish, Andrew E447
Vick, Charles W. E309
von Herwarth, Hans Wolfgang E421 E524

Wall, Bernhardt E429
Ward, Lock and Co. E165 E173 E174 E219 E266 E409
Warne, F. and Co. E201 E209 E212 E224
Warner, P. L. E400
Weaver, Bennet D30
Whiting, Lilian E408 E413
Whitney, G. C. E199
Whittaker, Thomas E57 E68
Winston, J. C. Company E382
Wise, Thomas J. B1 B2 B4 B5 B6 B7 B9 B11 B12 B13 B14 B15
Wood, Edmund S. E527
Worthington E117 E144 E167 E168 E184 E185 E187 E192 E204

Yale University Press D35

Zetlin, Michael E510

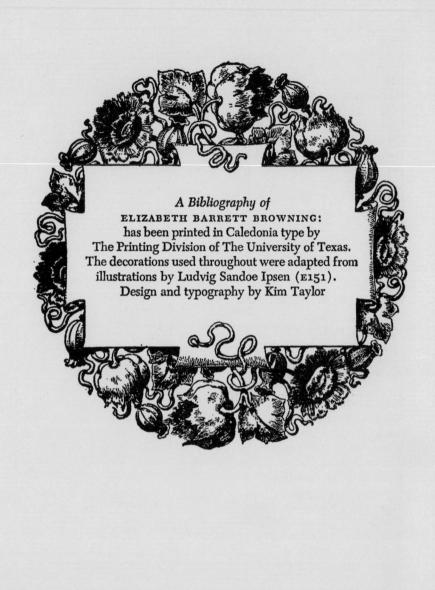

A Bibliography of
ELIZABETH BARRETT BROWNING:
has been printed in Caledonia type by
The Printing Division of The University of Texas.
The decorations used throughout were adapted from
illustrations by Ludvig Sandoe Ipsen (E151).
Design and typography by Kim Taylor